The Bush Garden

Esther Wettenhall grew up in Geelong in a garden-loving family and her holidays were often spent in the old home of her grandparents in the Grampians. These times gave her a love of wild and rugged landscape and the delicate wildflowers that are a feature of these ranges.

After marrying at 22, she and her husband lived a city life with their two sons and two daughters. Her dreams of a bush garden had to be put on the back burner for some years until they found a half acre block at Mount Martha. This is the beginning of her story.

She started writing for the *Age* garden section at 60 and this, her first book, was written at 70 years of age.

She feels passionately about the thoughtless clearing of bush blocks where no attempt is made to preserve the existing native trees and plants, and sees the use of chemical sprays of every sort to be unnecessary.

Her book is designed to be read by all those who love the beauty and tranquillity of the natural world.

Ringtail pos

The
Bush Garden

Esther Wettenhall

HYLAND HOUSE

First published in 1995 by
Hyland House Publishing Pty Limited
Hyland House
387-389 Clarendon Street
South Melbourne
Victoria 3205

National Library of Australia
Cataloguing-in-publication data

Wettenhall, Esther.
  The bush garden.

  Includes index.
  ISBN 1 875657 35 5.

  1. Native plant gardens—Australia. 2. Native plant
  gardening—Australia. 3. Natural landscaping—Australia.
  4. Garden fauna—Australia. 5. Gardening to attract
  wildlife—Australia. I. Title.

635.95194

Drawings by Margaret Wright
Photographs by Bill Lester
Typeset by Solo Typesetting, South Australia
Printed by Toppan Printing Co. (S) Pte. Ltd.

Foreword

Chocolate lilies.

THE BEAUTY, SUBTLETY AND INTRICACIES OF THE AUSTRALIAN bush are something many Australians grow up with and often take for granted. To others they represent a whole new world of excitement and discovery through wanderings in the bush or by planting a range of native plants and watching as the magical web of nature evolves within our own selected environment.

Humans are not the only creatures on this planet, and maybe we are not even the most important. In addition to enjoying the presence of insects, birds and other animals around us, there is much to be admired in their lifestyles and a great deal we can learn, if only we take time to look and listen. All animal life is totally dependent on plants for its existence, and here again there is a diversity which is both fascinating and mind-boggling.

I am constantly amazed at developments in electronics and

computerisation, but can be equally stunned by the miracles of nature which are all around us.

In this delightful book we are taken along pathways which can excite fond memories of the past and also be an inspiration for future activities. Young readers and new gardeners will find a wealth of information on the pleasures of living with nature, and the establishment of native gardens. For Australian landscape design students it should certainly be recommended reading.

I thank Esther Wettenhall for sharing her knowledge and experiences with us all. It is a truly delightful book which begs to be read outdoors in spring or summer, near a pond or a birdbath and under the cool shade of a large tree.

GWEN ELLIOT

Coral pea.

Contents

Acknowledgements

Brunonia australis.

MY HEARTFELT GRATITUDE IS OFFERED TO MARGARET Wright and Bill Lester who have contributed most generously to the making of this book: Margaret with her delicate and delightful water colour paintings and Bill with his sensitive and detailed photographs.

To my sister-in-law, Joan Good, also I owe a great debt. Not only did she type the entire manuscript (and variations of it) but she kept an eagle eye on my propensity to purple prose.

Finally to my friend Moira Robinson many thanks for her helpful criticism and support.

Prologue

Dampiera so blue!

AT THE OUTSET OF THIS BOOK, I MUST ADMIT TO A MINOR passion for the Australian bush, from which I draw deep inspiration. At the same time, I make no pretensions to be an expert in any study of its flowers, trees, birds or insects. I offer a chronicle of experiences, glorious surprises, some successes, mine and other people's, mistakes I have made and suggestions for growing a bush garden.

Gardens are a microcosm of enormous interest and even the most uninspired examples usually support a variety of living forms from the humble ant (industrious would be a better word) to birds and bees.

Enormous strides have been made in the recognition of the beauty of Australian plants, but we have still a hang-up from our English and European backgrounds. We like to tame the wild. It is lovely to see the designer's hand shaping a garden, but let it be a gentle hand that works with nature, not against it.

The more one considers a garden to belong not only to us, but to a whole world of other living creatures, the more absorbing and fascinating the planning and growing of such a garden becomes.

Yellow robin,
one of our favourite birds.

To the memory of Peter
and
for my children
Priscilla
Simon
Sarah
and
Stephen

Bush Roots

1

Correa reflexa.

THERE IS AN INSTINCT IN HUMANS, I BELIEVE, TO PLANT and grow things. Maybe it has been stifled in many of us due to the life we are called upon to lead but, given the opportunity and the right set of circumstances, I think we are all gardeners at heart.

I wonder sometimes who was the first person to grow a plant for its beauty and not for its food value. What a revolutionary step! I suspect it might have been a woman who grew tired of being strictly practical. Maybe she wanted something sweet smelling to tuck in her hair or maybe she wanted to plant a bright flower at the door of her hut. Whoever or however it was, what an avalanche of beauty and what an industry this first step launched.

As a child, my siblings and I were taken for picnics to the bush, but my memory of such occasions is not one of joyous recollection.

Due to the fact that I suffered from car sickness, the whole outing was viewed with dread. The pleasure of rambling in the bush was marred by the ghastly prospect of the drive home. However, this was only one part of our introduction to the bush.

My mother's parents had retired from the land and built a home in the Grampians at the foot of Mount Cassell. Here the bush consisted of gums, wattles and the myriad wildflowers for which the Grampians are famous. My grandmother was ahead of her time in her appreciation and love of the Australian plants. Throughout her garden she grew many natives amongst the exotic flowers. In the spring she would arrange great vases of Australian flowers, filling the rooms with the sharp, sweet scent of mint and wattle, while trails of purple hardenbergia and white clematis hung from the mantelpieces. The garden had a creek flowing through it which at one point had been widened to form a pond with an island in the middle. Beside the creek was a great chestnut tree which seemed immense to me. In the May holidays we would go to stay in this paradise, collecting chestnuts in their polished glossy coats to pop by the fire at night and picking late apples from the orchard to crunch in our young, strong teeth. Passionfruit and muscatel grapes were trained along the verandah and I well remember the delicious smell at breakfast as we cut and ate the passionfruit laced with cream. The disused tennis court was used for a fowl run and, when we were getting in the way, our aunt would gently suggest that we should go and circulate the chooks. The theory was that a bit of exercise was good for the egg production, which just might have been a convenient myth.

A conventional circular drive wound round a lawn in front of the house, with paths leading out from it to distant parts of the garden. A summerhouse with rustic seats on each side overarched a path on which we sedately rode our horses. As I was rather small and young, my first steed was a half-Clydesdale, guaranteed not to do anything alarming such as getting skittish and tossing me off. However, I think he had a rather sly sense of humour. My first solo ride ended badly. As my steering was clearly not sufficiently authoritarian, this great, gentle beast plodded purposefully towards the summerhouse, scraping me off as he passed through.

Everywhere you looked were great trees, a range of mountains

False sarsaparilla.

Greenhood orchids.

stretching right across the skyline behind the house and a view to the distant lakes from the front of the house. Each day we would climb the mountains searching for wildflowers, exploring little creeks and rock pools garlanded with ferns. Pink and white heath grew up to our waists and higher. The lovely, glowing red *Correa reflexa*, *Astroloma conostephioides* (red flame heath), the tiny *Astroloma humifusum*, whose berries are relished by the emu, and many other wildflowers created a natural garden beautiful beyond belief, even though we were there in late autumn.

On other days we would walk through a neighbour's block to visit friends on the other side. Their block was totally untouched bush, where wildlife lived in complete safety. Quite often we would hear the drumming sound of emus' feet as they ran through the bush. As a child I was a little apprehensive about this wildness and feared being run down by an emu. Sadly, the lovely old home in the Grampians was totally destroyed in the catastrophic bush fires of Black Friday 1939, but the influences and the memories linger on.

In Australia an increasing awareness of our heritage gardens has led people to visit many historic homes. In these gardens that have been tended and loved for over a century there is a strong feeling of history.

The gardens of two of my great-grandparents are still in existence after 154 years and are cared for by their descendants. Fire and storm have done their best to destroy first one and then the other, but the gardens have survived, their great old trees a testament to the vision of their planters. Many of the plants and trees in one old garden are from other lands, set in a framework of Australian bush, the home paddocks are dotted with gum trees which come up to the garden fences. The other garden, part of a working farm, was planted by a gardener who valued both Australian and exotic plants.

Subconsciously, holidays, spent in such lovely bush surroundings, were weaving a spell upon me, from which I have never escaped. I say to those who would grow a bush garden, go out into the lovely wild places of our land. Study the way things grow and relate to their surroundings. While we can never create anything as natural, we can absorb the feel of it and reproduce in our sterile suburbs a miniature bush garden that will attract an amazing variety of birds, insects and other life forms.

In the Beginning 2

An importunate magpie.

FROM EARLY CHILDHOOD DAYS, I DREAMED OF HAVING A large garden of my own. In my mind it was an amalgam of the Grampians, those great rocky fortresses whose sides are swathed in garlands of delicate wildflowers; the Dandenong Ranges, their moist gullies filled with ferns and the ringing calls of the lyrebird; and the coastal heathland, with its sweeping sea views and golden sands. I thought big in those days.

As I grew older, my dreams contracted to a more manageable size and a small piece of bush seemed a lovely but unattainable wish which perhaps might be fulfilled one day. As happens in life, one Sunday morning found my husband Peter and me hunting the Land for Sale columns in the paper, under Country Properties. The reading of advertisements was an addiction to which we were prone, fantasising about throwing up our city life and taking up subsistence living on a small farm. Mercifully, we never realised this fantasy.

On discovering a small block of land for sale at a very reasonable price on the Mornington Peninsula, we packed the children and a picnic lunch into the car and sallied forth. The area held an immediate attraction to us, as much courting and many happy times had been spent in this environment.

The unmade road down which we drove had only two houses on it and the rest of the land consisted of tea-tree, she-oaks, eucalypts and wattles. Now, to find the block. Several of the lots looked bare, but when we reached the designated one we saw, with much delight, groves of she-oaks and several eucalypts. It was a half-acre block with vacant land all round and, across the road, down in the gully ran a creek, a haven for the birds. It took two minutes to decide on the purchase and, thanks to a small legacy, our dream became a reality.

One year and a new baby later, our three-bedroomed little weatherboard house was completed. Our delightful builder, an ex-ship's carpenter, was a lively Glaswegian of impenetrable accent, who entered into our shoestring approach to building with enthusiasm and had no difficulty in constructing the house from second-hand weatherboards, the gift of a friend. He kept us endlessly amused and, although we were never quite sure whether we were giving the right responses to some of his remarks, we all got along fine. He loved the 'babby' and, being a bachelor with no children of his own, he liked to hold him and talk to him in his inimitable accent. Apart from his very reasonable charges for building the house, he was very generous about doing other things for us. He towed our rather large and cumbersome caravan, which had been reposing at the bottom of the block, up and across the perilously bumpy neighbouring block. We watched in terror as the whole lurching edifice made its way over mounds and hidden potholes, until it came to rest safely at the back of the cottage. There it remained for some years as overflow accommodation for friends and family.

The builder's brother-in-law, a kind and proficient bricklayer from Aberdeen with an easier accent to grasp, built us a splendid open fireplace in the living room, which we surmounted with a black and white marble mantelpiece. This we had bought for a song when a neighbouring house in Armadale was being pulled down. Being unable to resist such a bargain, but having no immediate use for it, it resided rather incongruously in our

Native fuchsia.

Prickly tea-tree.

Coastal banksia.

lavatory, leaving very little elbow room, until such time as a use could be found for it. Keep a thing long enough . . . !

The bricklayer had a dear wife who, when she heard that I had become ill, rang to enquire whether she could look after the 'babby' for me until I was fully recovered. I have never forgotten her kindness.

As there was no water, gas or electricity, a second-hand slow combustion stove was installed on which to cook and to provide us with hot water. Two large rainwater tanks, completed our needs.

After ransacking junk shops for lanterns and finding glass chimneys for them, we spent a happy few years there on holiday and weekends, playing games by lantern light as reading was a little difficult. It makes one realise how spoilt we are with electric light. I can't imagine how fine sewing, let alone reading, was done in olden times, sometimes with only a candle to illumine the work.

The little house nestled on its slope, looking into the trees from every window. Kookaburras and magpies soon became regular visitors as did ravens, rosellas and many other birds. The kookaburras became quite tame and would alight on the verandah railing to accept proffered pieces of raw meat. The magpies were even more at ease with us and used to tap imperiously on the windows, demanding to be fed.

In the summer we had several visits from copperhead snakes, whose territory we had invaded. I regret to say that we despatched them, something we would try to avoid if possible these days. However, with a young child wandering in the long grasses one's high principles about protecting wildlife tend to weaken. Occasionally wallabies bounded up the adjacent block or an odd echidna wandered through, looking preoccupied with the business of navigating his way, and blue-tongue lizards appeared on hot summer days.

We felt very rural indeed, but kept a nervous eye on the block next door. Might a yuppie buy it and build a horrific house right on the boundary overseeing our little haven? When eventually it did come on the market, we heard of it immediately. Without pausing for a second, we accepted the asking price and became the proud owners of another half-acre block. Behold, we were now the undisputed owners of a bit of bush! My yearning for a big garden, though somewhat less than the original prospect, had been granted.

Aims and Aspirations 3

A nosey echidna.

WITH THE ADDITION OF ANOTHER HALF-ACRE OF LAND, WE now had scope to try and put into practice some of our ideas.

There was not much to be said for the new block. It was covered in viciously sharp-bladed sword grass, had a few small she-oaks, one large *Acacia decurrens* (black wattle) and one small *Eucalyptus viminalis* (manna gum), but now it was part of an extended garden and so ripe for conversion into a bush garden which would be inhabited, so we hoped, by many creatures.

Broadly our aims for the garden included preserving the environment with its mystical element, exploring the potential of bush flowers, introducing water for the birds and insects whilst being niggardly with watering the plants, and understanding and promoting the ecology.

Making a bush garden which encourages all forms of native

life, including the human species, either to remain in it or to return to it, is an exciting challenge which can become a lifetime's obsession. It does not exclude, if so desired, the introduction of plants from other lands sympathetic to the design and the environment. Most of the great gardens of the world contain intriguing and beautiful plants from other countries, but in bush gardens care must be taken not to introduce a jarring note of exoticism. I am not a purist and confess to bouts of 'mania exotica' when temptation gets the better of me. I find it difficult to resist the charms of roses, irises and small daisies to mention just a few, but these are largely planted as a frill around the house.

There are often many obstacles to contend with which are an end product of land degradation caused by clearing trees, spraying with herbicides or pesticides and the introduction of unsuitable, invasive plants. Most of us tend to plant things that grow easily, hence plants such as agapanthus, arum lilies, gazanias and ixias become, not only a cliché, but runaway pests, usurping the places of gentler and more suitable flowers.

A bush garden is not for those who love tidiness and neatness, nor is it a place of continuous bright colour. Although tropical gardens wear a many-coloured cloak at all seasons of the year, most of the Australian bush gardens have seasonal bursts of colour which are separated by times of changing green hues and wildflowers of infinite charm. These are not conspicuously showy, Western Australian varieties being the exception. A small bush garden can become an intimate, romantic and private world for lovers of nature and for lovers. Native grasses that are allowed to remain unmown beneath the trees, in combination with fallen leaves form a soft carpet on which to lie, looking up at the sky through a canopy of gently moving leaves. There is much to observe on the ground as you lie relaxing in this quiet world. Continuous activity of ants, tiny insects and bugs of unknown name catch the eye as they go purposefully about their business, parting small blades of grass as they make their way through their own private jungle.

A bush garden is a place for dreaming dreams and not being harassed by our inherited notions of law and order. Nature makes her own laws if given her head, and the order she produces is one that is very different from our commonly held views.

Wedding bush.

Native grass.

Eggs and bacon.

The first rule in making a bush garden is to throw out any ideas of imposing our own will on our environment. If we insist on clipped edges, mown lawns, carefully placed statuary (not koalas, please) the whole point of growing a bush garden is lost. If we continue to tidy up every fallen branch, rotted log or scatter of twigs and leaves, we are doing three things. First, we are starving the garden of a natural food source obtained from the rotting down process. Second, we are removing a protective mulch which conserves precious moisture in the soil and protects small herbs and wildflowers. Third, we are invading and destroying the territory of many species of creatures, who perform a specific role in the ecology of the bush.

Initially, it takes a bit of courage to actively promote what appears to be chaos, but after your bush garden has had a year or so to establish itself, you will really get the hang of it. If you are starting from scratch, that is an empty and treeless block, go for some quick growing trees to give the area a focus. Trees such as *Acacia floribunda*, which are semi-weeping, grow at a great rate outward as well as upward and in a few years, with a little judicious shaping, will give you an outdoor room just the perfect place to take tea. To be enclosed by sweet-smelling wattle blossom has a lot to recommend it.

Our first job on the new land was to subdue and largely get rid of the sword grass which covered the block. It took only one thoughtless pull at the blades with bare hands, to impress on us its vicious cutting edge and the necessity for sturdy gloves. With two ancient sickles we hacked our way up and down the slope, reducing the task to manageable proportions. As we started planting trees, we dug out the grass in a wide area around each little tube and mulched heavily. There was ample mulch to be had from under the she-oaks and tea-trees which abounded in the area. The leaves of both these trees make a perfect mulch for native plants.

As the land sloped down from back to front, we had that most precious attribute, good drainage, which for many native plants is essential. There are, of course, many swamp-loving trees and plants too for those whose gardens have intractable wet areas.

As we did not intend to bring in topsoil, which would be alien to the environment, our first aim was to plant indigenous trees. These consisted of *Acacia pycnantha*, the golden wattle and emblem of Australia, and *A. suaveolens*, a sweetly scented small wattle; *Allocasuarina littoralis* and *A. verticillata*; two forms of banksia, *B. integrifolia* and *B. marginata*; and three forms of eucalypt, *Eucalyptus ovata*, *E. pauciflora* and *E. viminalis*, all preferred forms of breakfast for the koala. Along with these, we planted tea-trees and many small rooted suckers of *Melaleuca ericifolia*, which is liked by the ringtail possum for nesting.

Having established a framework of local trees and discovered small she-oaks and wattles seeding in the garden, we started devouring books and catalogues about Australian plants that would thrive in our poor granitic soil. To our delight, many of the wildflowers which we found growing in the area were favourites from childhood holidays in the Grampians.

We were anxious to attract as many birds as possible to the garden, so our first purchases were grevilleas. The range of these plants is huge and we found that almost without exception, every variety we planted flourished, although I must say that *Grevillea robusta*, that glorious tall tree with its golden flowers, has taken an unconscionably long time to grow. The blue-flowered *G. shiressii*, supposed to be irresistible to the honeyeaters, has grown like a flash, looks remarkably healthy, never has a bird in it and sports so far in its life span two almost invisible blue flowers, which I think the birds must find as difficult to discover as I do. Well, you can't win them all and I tell myself that *G. shiressii* is interesting and unusual.

The more we read books on Australian flowers, the more we were won over by their unique charm and most visits to that most mundane of all necessary evils, the supermarket, found us searching the native plants section for small plants which were appropriate choices for our garden. Tucked in with the groceries, this was a barely noticeable indulgence.

Beetles, bugs and little lizards were catered for by the introduction into the garden of rocks and rotting logs and, to our great excitement, we had more visits from an echidna for whom there were plenty of ants. A delightful lizard, who looked like a little dragon and ran on his back legs, shinned up the she-oak trunks with alacrity, then remained motionless surveying his world.

Despite the fact that so much of the surrounding bush with its unique plants and creatures has gone, due to an expansion of building, our acre continues to support a wide variety of bush life. Shrubs, trees and grasses seed and our private jungle continues to grow, kept in check by the inevitable death of some of the trees. Our aspirations have been met and our pleasure is unmitigated.

Rooms with a View 4

Golden whistler
with young.

EEKENDS SPENT IN THE LITTLE HOUSE AND WORKING
on the two blocks became more and more special.
We found it increasingly difficult to tear ourselves away
from the peace and unspoilt beauty of our surroundings. With a
certain amount of recklessness, we decided to build a permanent
and roomier house on the second block and come to live here,
keeping the little house for our grown-up children and their
friends. As our young son was only just nine, it was not a
traumatic time for him to change schools and I think he was
pretty impressed at the thought of living by the sea.

A great designer of environmental houses, Alastair Knox, drew
plans for a house that suited us perfectly and he came down to
site it on the block. The first major upheaval was caused by the
bulldozer, which had to level the site. Due to the slope of the
land and the fact that the house was to be built on a concrete

slab, two levels had to be excavated. At our request, the driver of the bulldozer took great care to avoid knocking down the few trees which were growing close to the house site, and he piled the topsoil in one huge heap for us to use later. As we waved him goodbye at the end of the day, he drove off in his juggernaut down the steep road. Suddenly we heard with alarm the roar of increasing speed and muffled shouts. Racing down the drive, we were horrified to see the bulldozer hurtling backwards off the road into the trees and bushes leading down to the gully. It finally came to rest on an acute angle and we were thankful to see the driver still clinging to the wheel, white-faced but unharmed.

The materials used for the construction of the house were old, handmade bricks of varying shades of warm apricot. Tasmanian oak was used to line some of the walls and second-hand red gum timbers were used for the interior posts, steps and rails. This may sound rather dark and heavy, but in fact the house is light, spacious and uncluttered. Due to clerestory windows and vast amounts of floor to ceiling glass windows and doors, there is a strong feeling of affinity with the garden.

Sited with its back into the slope and facing north, the eaves keep out the hot summer sun, but winter sun floods the rooms. The slate floors are deliciously cool to bare feet in the hot weather and in the winter they are warmed by under-floor pipes of hot water. Open fireplaces in two rooms give a warm greeting in the winter months as they crackle and sparkle with an abundance of twigs, branches and boughs of wood from fallen trees.

For a garden to be worth its salt, it is surely just as important that it be seen from inside the house, as from the outside. To shut oneself away from all that beauty is to deny half the joy of gardening and lose a dimension of living. When planning a house, it seems to me that a great deal of thought should be given to the direction the windows face and what can be seen through them. Having a bird-attracting shrub or tree and a birdbath close to the window where you most commonly sit, is to experience the endless pleasure of watching the antics and general busyness of birds' lives.

As I write, I am constantly being distracted by the activity taking place in two bird pools close to the windows. In one, a birdbath sitting on the cut-down trunk of a she-oak, there is a

Author's room with a view.

Yellow and pink boronias.

congestion of birds all jockeying for position in the water. While yellow-winged honeyeaters have a reputation for being bullies, seven of them are sharing their bath with four white-naped honeyeaters in perfect amity. The only competition appears to be between who can shimmy and shake the best. In the other bath a solitary yellow-winged honeyeater and a white-naped honeyeater share their bath with total decorum.

If it is the colour and form of flowers that bring you the greatest joy, plant them where they can be seen from every window — a riot of colour or soft muted tones can do much to raise the spirit. Looking from the house down a garden slope that combines grass, native trees, shrubs and other plants, there is always something to observe. When it is raining outside and a gale is blowing, I feel I am part of the garden with its wildly waving branches and birds flying helter-skelter through the sky. Adding to this feeling of delight is the smug snugness of toasting one's toes by a cheery fire.

Although bathrooms tend to be the smallest rooms in the house, there seem few reasons why they should not command a view that could inspire even the most jaded of us at the start of the day. If you don't pine for one of those amazing and spacious bathrooms with sunken baths and mirrored walls designed to give you uninterrupted contemplation of the nude figure, I re-commend a view such as my bathroom windows afford. As I stand towelling briskly after my cold shower, it is pleasant to look up the slope through a light screen of tea-tree, grevillea, *Hakea sericea* — whose flowers create a pink mist in winter — and melaleuca, to the pond. Although it is not possible to see the water from the window, the visits of the eastern rosella are clearly visible as he sits preening his bright feathers after a dunk in the water. Many other birds visit the pond, so there is a good chance of seeing some bird performing its ablutions whilst I perform mine. If you have a blank wall to look out on, grow a clinging creeper on it, or hang baskets of flowers and trailing plants — anything that provides a vision of beauty growing and blooming.

Bedrooms, where we spend a third of our lives, should be rooms of great charm, inside and out. The interior of a bedroom is an intensely personal choice, but I love to feel that in my bedroom I am almost sleeping in the bush, without the accompanying drawbacks of spiders, mosquitoes, prowling wild animals (not the hissing, roaring types) and the vagaries of the weather. Wakening in the morning to see, just outside the window, the sun shining on the leaves or the rain staining the trunks of the trees, is a peaceful way to start the day.

The pleasure of low-set windows is that the eye follows the garden without interruption; hence it becomes an extension of the house. If existing windows cannot be lowered, then plant something that will grow tall enough to be seen from inside, not a dense tree that excludes light, but one that combines delicacy with seasonal interest. However, one has to be careful not to plant anything close to the house that can cause problems for pipes or foundations, such as an early mistake we made, when the house was in danger of being uprooted by an over-large eucalypt. Some shrubs which are shapely and colourful, and can be planted safely near underground pipes, include *Acacia buxifolia*, *A. drummondii*, *A. myrtifolia* and *A. pulchella*. Correas, croweas, and eremophila, eriostemon, eutaxia and many grevilleas are amongst middle-sized attractive shrubs, as are *Boronia fraseri*, *B. heterophylla* and *B. pinnata*. Olearias, prostantheras and westringias are all hardy and there are many smaller plants such as *Bauera rubioides* and *B. sessiflora*, *Thomasia petalocalyx*, and members of the epacris and helichrysum family, which can be grown without a care in the vicinity of pipes.

In the kitchen, where one usually works standing up, windows can be set higher, but they are of great importance to the cook. Preparing a meal or washing dishes becomes a positive pleasure for those of us who don't find culinary chores one of life's greater joys, if we can stand at a window gazing into the garden as we work.

From the kitchen window, we look out onto a fairly wild, semi-circular thicket. Here the flowering *Hibbertia scandens* makes splashes of colour from its wide-open yellow flowers, as it climbs through *Eremophila glabra* (emu bush) and the mauve-flowered *Thomasia petalocalyx*. This plant has attractive, soft-felt leaves and the mauve 'petals' are really the calyx of the flower. It grows to a good sized bush and is hardy in our garden, even seeding into the uncongenial ground of the driveway. As it is inclined to rampage, the hibbertia must be kept away from the *Grevillea endlicherana*, whose graceful arching stems of small leaves bear wispy pink flowers. Underneath the grevillea grows a pink *Correa reflexa*, whose pink bells have pale green reflexed petals, the prostrate *Myoporum parvifolium*, which is covered in white, starry flowers in spring, and the pink *Thryptomene saxicola*—the white *T. calycina*, which grows in such profusion in the Grampians, is not overfond of our soil. The slender and shapely *Acacia paradoxa*, which has fiendish prickles, in company with a handsome, flowering *Eutaxia microphylla*, make a vivid splash of yellow in spring on the lower bank of the thicket, while a little indigenous yellow-flowered *Hibbertia stricta* grows at the foot of the wattle beside a large clump of reeds and rounded rock. An upended root of a large tree makes a good stand for a birdbath, with its rooty arms as convenient perches for curious birds. It blends into the surroundings better than a formal type of bird table and the pool in its grasp is a constant source of interest.

The background of the kitchen view is made up of a framework of tall casuarinas, tea-trees and a dead black wattle, whose attenuated form is greatly favoured by a variety of birds, who use it for perching, preening, overseeing the territory, or just temporarily resting.

The rough lawn outside the kitchen window and the thick jasmine clothing one verandah post is a favourite area for that most jaunty and adorable of little birds, the blue wren, whose bevy of women folk and irrepressible small fry always seem to outnumber him by about five to one. I never feel shut out from life when working in the kitchen, even if there are no humans about.

Whether in an established or a new garden, it shouldn't be too difficult to make areas of colour, life, scent and sound, that can be seen and enjoyed from every room in the house.

Planting Round the House 5

A visitor on the clematis.

WITH HOUSES THAT ARE BUILT ON CONCRETE SLABS there is always the problem of dealing with the excavated soil. As our land sloped, the soil was levelled out in front of the house to form a terrace and the topsoil carefully preserved in a separate heap for us to use in making the terrace garden. Before we had time to more than vaguely map out our plans for the area, a pair of spotted pardalotes had discovered the pile of sandy topsoil and moved in with alacrity to build their home. The spotted pardalote is one of the smallest and brightest of our little birds. Its charming little three note piping call is clearly heard although it is sometimes difficult to see high up in the trees. It gets its insect food mainly from the surface of leaves and a leaf is sufficient to hide it from view.

From a small opening in the soil they dug out a little tunnel, at the end of which was their nest. From just inside their front door they would take stock of the outside world before darting out at high speed to go about their business. It was several months before our pardalotes had reared their family and decided to move on. Then, and only then, could we begin to make our terrace garden, but they were such a joy to watch, we didn't begrudge them the time spent waiting.

In our hurry to clothe the naked posts holding up the overhanging roof, we planted *Jasminum polyanthum*, greatly loved for its delicious scent, *Hardenbergia violacea*, for its long-lasting season of purple flowers through winter to spring and *Kennedia rubicunda* for its vigorous growth and attraction for the birds. *Grevillea* 'Poorinda Firebird' and G. 'Clearview David' were also planted and became irresistible to the eastern spinebill. It was a delight to sit by the window and watch the incessant activity of this most elegant of small honeyeaters. With its rufous tan and black and white colouring, its long curved beak and its whirring wings, it is difficult to tear one's glance away as it probes the flowers for nectar.

As with many mistakes in life, it is hard to admit to them and it was many years before we grudgingly admitted that the kennedia had taken over, shading completely one end of the open verandah and interfering dangerously with the power lines and guttering. If we had used more forethought or perhaps willpower, we would have kept it well pruned back. Maybe this would have saved its life, but be warned, it is a very vigorous, rampageous climber like its brother, *Kennedia nigricans*. We replaced the kennedia with *Billardiera erubescens*, a much more delicate native creeper, which has clusters of red/orange little bells through spring and summer and presents no problems.

The jasmine is a source of both joy and rage—joy in its endless flowers and sweet scent, and rage at its undisciplined behaviour. It has clothed the post quite charmingly but sends out enormous runners that climb through anything and everything, strangling precious plants as it goes on its merry way. It layers and sends down roots which is great if you like to pull them up and give them away, always of course, warning the recipient of its wicked ways. Again, if we had been more regularly ruthless in cutting it back right from the start, the rampage could have been contained. There is still time.

Another near mistake was the planting of the hardenbergia. It has grown strongly and again was not cut back. It developed a dry, dead and twiggy centre but, just as we were about to apply surgery, we discovered a ringtail possum's nest in its interior so it remains untidy but intact for its rightful owner.

At the base of the post up which climbs the billardiera, we planted a *Grevillea* 'Robyn Gordon' and on the other side of the post at the edge of the brick paving, we planted a French lavender bush. In days of old, lavender walks were common in big gardens and ladies in their long skirts strolled between the lavender bushes, their skirts brushing the fragrant flowers. The idea has always appealed to me and, whilst not commonly dressed in long skirts, I do manage to brush frequently against the sweet smelling bush. Bees, of course, love lavender and are usually in attendance, but have a benign nature and are far too busy about their own affairs to cause any disturbance to us humans. ''Tis the melancholy face that gets bit by the bee!' The old-fashioned gift of a homemade lavender bag is always received with pleasure and is guaranteed to bring fragrance to your drawers. If placed under your pillow, maybe it will bring sweet dreams.

The 'Robyn Gordon' on the other side of the post is one of the most generous of the grevilleas and is practically never without flowers. The long red trusses are constantly visited by all the honeyeaters in the garden and provide a welcome splash of colour the year round.

Three large rounded volcanic rocks were given to me for a birthday present and placed with great care near the climbing jasmine. Planted beside them is a clump of *Diplarrena moraea*, a native white-flowering iris with flat thin leaves. It multiplies itself by layering the long arching stems, which take root readily as they reach the ground. The purple-flowering native iris, *Patersonia occidentalis*, is another showy plant widespread in Australia. It is seen at its best in damp but sunny areas and flowers from October to January. It is a plant of the coastal heathland and also looks well amongst rocks.

In roughly delineated small beds around the posts, a certain amount of impulse planting goes on. *Viola hederacea*, the native violet, which has naturalised in large areas around the garden has had to be dug out to make room for lovable exotics like a very old-fashioned rose which was given to me as a cutting. It has clusters of sweet pink flowers, anything up to ninety at a time, and is recurrent. Its name is 'Poulsen's Pink Pearl' and it is hard to find these days. Beside this is a pure white rose, grown from a cutting of the deservedly popular 'Iceberg'. There are several other exotics which, for sentimental reasons, are allowed to co-exist in our largely native garden. They are restricted to an area close to the house and not permitted to encroach on the wild garden, the criterion for their presence being that they do not look incongruous in their surroundings.

Sowing grass on the rather poor soil of the terrace, with its thin layer of topsoil, was our next concern. At the time native grass seed was not obtainable, so we bought a tough mixture of seed including some clover, which we knew would sweeten the soil. It took us some years to realise that we were making a rod for our own backs with the necessary watering and feeding of this alien grass. We let it die and gradually, with the help of handfuls of dry seed heads of native grass and a refusal to water, we have now created a soft cover of grass, which we mow only occasionally and never water. We were slow learners but got there in the end. We now acknowledge that a bright green manicured lawn looks inappropriate in a bush garden and with the help of *Dichondra repens*, a small mat plant, and the native violet, we have a natural looking terrace lawn.

Planting the bank was our next endeavour and here we had some successes. The indigenous *Melaleuca ericifolia* was planted in a small clump. This grew quickly and sent up suckers, so that in a couple of years we had a small copse, with papery bark beginning to develop on the trunks. The soft cream flowers bloom profusely in spring and the tree grows best in a moist situation with full or partial shade. As it was growing at the base of the bank, it received plenty of moisture. At the foot of the melaleuca we planted the little slender twining *Billardiera scandens*, another indigenous plant, commonly called climbing appleberry. This twines or sprawls and has greenish yellow bells, singly or in twos amongst the leaves.

Clematis microphylla, another quick-growing indigenous climber, was also planted so as to wind its way up the melaleuca, as it does so often in the wild. It creates a feathery light effect with its four-petalled white flowers, followed by an effusion of fluffy seed heads, giving it the name of old man's beard. As with most plants, pruning will promote its bushy growth, but for my money it has more charm being allowed its freedom. Small birds

Kangaroo paw.

Grevillea 'Poorinda Firebird'.

such as grey fantails and thornbills tend to swing on the slender, looping stems of the plant, before diving into a nearby pool of water.

From many helichrysums (everlastings) we chose to plant *Helichrysum bracteatum* (straw flower), whose yellow flowers bloom over a long period; clumps of yellow *Helichrysum apiculatum*, the local everlasting, and seedings of *Helipterum manglesii*. This is an annual species of everlasting daisy with papery flowers of shades of pink and white, which can be picked and dried off to make colourful bunches of indoor flowers. Although it is an annual, the windblown seeds tend to pop up in succeeding years, although the flowers gradually become miniature editions of their forbears.

A small plant of *Anigozanthos flavidus* (kangaroo paw) was placed at the bottom of the bank and has done spectacularly. It gets plenty of sun and enough moisture to keep it happy. It has developed over many years into a large clump, with long stems producing long-lasting soft velvety red and green flowers. Viewing this from the house is a constant attraction, or should I say distraction, as it is frequently visited by the honeyeaters. The wattle bird plunges in and rides the flower stem to the ground as it gorges on the nectar. When sated it flies off and the bent stem springs up again. The eastern spinebill has a more elegant approach to feeding and delicately probes the kangaroo paws for its refreshment. Although this plant is Western Australian, it does seem to be very adaptable to other areas and in our bush garden it is not only hardy, but has self-seeded too, which is exciting. When any native plant seeds in my garden I take it as a compliment and an indication that the bush is reasserting its rightful place. This is not to say that, as in life, there are not some who are too self-assertive. *Pittosporum undulatum* and *Sollya heterophylla* are two plants which tend to put themselves forward overmuch and have to be disciplined quite firmly.

The indigenous heath *Epacris impressa*, whilst widespread in the bush, is more difficult to retain. One or two plants have survived for quite a few years, but others have come and gone in a matter of two years. The soil and conditions would appear to be perfect, but there is no accounting for the waywardness of some plants; maybe there are too many trees.

Boronias are another plant which succeed and fail in equal proportions. After many trials, I have decided to treat *Boronia megastigma*, that sweet scented Western Australian, as an annual and, instead of buying a bunch of its irresistible flowers in springtime, I buy a plant of it and enjoy its perfume in the garden, always with the hope that it may survive a few seasons. It is said to do well in bog gardens, so is well worth trying if you have that sort of situation. *Boronia anemonifolia, B. fraseri* and *B. muelleri* are three boronias suited to shady, dry positions and are surviving well in our bush garden, whilst *B. heterophylla* grows to a large bush, bearing bright pink bells in spring. Both leaves and flowers are sweetly scented. It is a very rapid grower, responds well to pruning and has been known even to survive the depredations of an undisciplined digging dog.

Tucked into the bank are several plants of *Brachyscome multifida* (cutleaf daisy). This is a sprawling bushy little plant, hardy, widespread and long-flowering. The daisy flowers are lilac, fading to pink and white, and cover the bush. As I write, I am watching clouds of butterflies drifting about the bank. Although they are not fast fliers, they spend very little time sipping at each flower they visit. Either they cannot get sufficient nectar from a few flowers, or they are picky eaters. They seem to be in perpetual slow motion, which lends a dreamlike quality to their flight.

In order to be able to walk down the bank to the lower garden in something less than an undignified scramble, we made a pathway in three places, cut several wide shallow steps held by logs of wood, and planted clumps of reeds, native irises, *Correa reflexa* and *Crowea exalata* to soften the edges. A large terracotta dish was placed on a stump beside the path for a bird pool and very soon the little wild violets and *Dichondra repens* had moved in to form a walking mat.

As the plants on the bank come and go, we have identified some long-lasting beauties which have defied death and destruction from drought, falling trees and injudicious watering. Of the many Australian heaths, *Epacris longiflora* has been one of the outstanding successes in our garden. Our criteria for success are hardiness and long-flowering seasons. In fact, *Epacris longiflora* is practically never without flowers and the beauty of its deep, rose pink bells, tipped with white, and borne on long arching sprays is a source of joy both to us and to the honeyeaters. Its natural habitat is open forest, a habitat to which our bush garden aspires.

6 *Grassy Woodland*

A wandering Ulysses butterfly.

THE DEFINITION OF WOODLAND IS AN AREA DOMINATED BY trees in open formation, where the foliage cover occupies 30 per cent or less of the ground. Grassy woodland is dominated by a grass understorey, in which other shrubs and a range of herbs may occur.

In the early days of white settlement on the Mornington Peninsula, the coast was heavily wooded with casuarinas. When it was discovered that the wood of the tree was long-burning and gave out much heat, the trees were cut down at a great rate and shipped off to Melbourne for use in the bakery kilns. Subsequent to this, where formerly there had been casuarina forests, tea-tree quickly established itself and became the dominant tree on the coast.

An example of the speed at which a local woodland can be degraded was the invasion of pine trees from a neighbouring pine plantation. The seedlings proliferated and at great speed overtook and smothered the natural growth of *Banksia marginata* in a little park owned and set aside by the Council for residents to enjoy.

Our young son, by now keenly interested in the environment, wrote to the Council offering to help get rid of the pine trees in order to facilitate the regrowth of indigenous plants. His letter was acknowledged with the promise of future action and within two years the whole area of pine trees had been felled. The metamorphosis is remarkable. Where once there was nothing to be seen but dreary pine trees, there is now a mass of banksias, some tea-tree, viminaria and many wildflowers including *Orthoceras strictum* (horned orchid) and native grasses. It is a joy to walk through. This is a success story.

A less happy event occurred when developers purchased a large tract of nearby open woodland, in which there was a big lake round which was a well used little track. Here couples took their evening stroll and children happily fished (if that is what it's called) for yabbies. This area had many huge old gum trees and was a place of birds.

Almost overnight as it seemed, the lake was drained, land fill was brought in and what had been a small paradise looked like a football field. My young grandson, who had spent many happy hours fishing for yabbies and then earnestly returning them to their watery environment, came home nearly in tears after seeing the destruction of the lake. It has gone and we are all the poorer.

In our grassy woodland the dominant indigenous trees are the wattles *Acacia melanoxylon*, *A. pycnantha* and *A. suaveolens*, *Allocasuarina littoralis*, *A. verticillata* (commonly known as she-oaks), *Banksia integrifolia* and *B. marginata*.

Of the many varieties of casuarina, that lovely and neglected species of tree, we have three in our garden, two of which are indigenous to the area. *Allocasuarina verticillata* is a leafless tree with drooping grey-green pine-like needles, which are in fact branchlets and act as leaves. It is common on the plains, rocky outcrops or in coastal areas. A tree of great hardiness and beauty, its male flowers of rusty yellow hang like velvet tassels at the end of the branchlet.

Allocasuarina littoralis is an erect dark green tree of 6 to 12 metres. Male and female flowers are borne on the same tree. As with *A. verticillata,* the male flower spikes are burnt ochre in colour, while the female flower is a small red floret glistening as with dew on the end of a tiny stem.

Allocasuarina torulosa is an erect tree with drooping rose-coloured tips to the branchlets and corky bark on the trunk. As with all casuarinas, it drops a litter of pine needles which are soft to walk on and which make perfect mulch for other native plants. To see a spider's web slung between the branches and sparkling with raindrops after a shower of rain, is to observe one of nature's miracles. As Alexander Pope expresses it:

'The spider's touch how exquisitely fine!

Feels at each thread, and lives along the line.'

The importance of trees in the garden cannot be over-emphasised. Many birds fly over our gardens without our being aware of their passing. Some are migratory birds on a long journey to a pre-determined destination, others are just tourists looking round to see what is offering and cleaning up any bargains that are available. Some are looking for territory in which to set up home, or to make a regular visit to feed. Whatever their motives, tall trees draw them like a magnet. If your garden or block has tall or middle-sized trees in it, such as casuarinas, eucalypts, wattles or any other native trees, treasure them. Go to extraordinary lengths to save them from destruction by cajoling and bullying builders, driveway designers and those who come to instal services of any sort, pointing out the contribution they are making to the preservation of beauty. In other words, butter them up!

We need trees to attract birds, insects and mammals. They also provide welcome shade in summer, a soothing, soughing sound at all seasons of the wind and a constant supply of fallen leaves, nuts, seed pods and twigs which nourish the soil.

On hearing a clatter in the bark of a gum tree, I go looking for the perpetrator of the noise, knowing for certain that I am going to see an eastern shrike-tit investigating the pantry shelves of his chosen tree. Digging with his beak, he extracts grubs and other small insects from the bark. His black crest sits up in sharp silhouette against the light and the dynamic colouring of his yellow, black and white markings make him a vivid visitor. Two other birds who frequent the garden also have this dramatic colouring. The joyous golden whistler has not only a melodious

Curtain of mistletoe.

Wild cherry.

Tranquillity in the garden.

and pure song, but his striking yellow and black markings, with a bib of pure white under his chin, stop you in your tracks as you spot him in the garden. The ubiquitous New Holland honeyeater is also the possessor of these colours. As he flashes about the grevilleas, in what can only be described as a bossy manner, the painted yellow enamelled splash on his wings is eye-catching. His call has something of the strident note associated with bullies the world over but, although he is flashy, he is gorgeous.

The dappled light and shade that spreads under our tall native trees gives a soft pattern to the ground underneath. It is a more gentle light than that of direct sunshine and throughout the four seasons the open canopy of our trees allows us to observe much of the activity of birds as they feed, preen and generally relax. In the tropical parts of Australia, it is much more difficult to see the birds, as the thick and lush vegetation makes a perfect cover for their movements. It is breathtaking to spot from the dark and mysterious depths of a rainforest garden, the emergence of a blue Ulysses butterfly, which floats over the garden with fragile grace, transfixing one with wonder.

It occurs to me sometimes, as I wander through the garden, that we spend too little time looking up into the trees. It is then that we discover that a tall eucalypt is bearing flowers on its crown, or that a patch of mistletoe is growing on the branch of a casuarina or eucalypt. *Amyema pendula*, the beautiful mistletoe with its red tasselled flowers, has long leathery leaves similar to a eucalypt and hangs in great bunches from the host tree.

The term parasite sounds pejorative, but in fact this is a natural phenomenon. The seed of the flower is eaten by the mistletoe bird, which digests the fleshy part and voids the seed, with its adhesive cover, onto the branch of a tree. It is from this living host that the seed draws its nourishment and quickly develops into a strong bunch of mistletoe securely attached to the tree. This, in time, is thought to lead to the death of the limb and ultimately the tree. What a dilemma! If we cut off the mistletoe, not only is the plant lost, but also the bonus of visits to the flowers from the exquisite little red, navy and white mistletoe bird. If we leave the mistletoe, we will eventually lose the tree. Coming down on the side of the natural order of things, the mistletoe gains a reprieve as we reflect thankfully that other casuarinas are springing up to replace their ageing relatives.

In 1839 an attempt was being made in the zoological gardens

of England to raise the seed of *Nuytsia floribunda*, commonly known in Western Australia as the Christmas tree, which blooms in November and December in great masses of vivid orange flowers. It also is a parasite of the mistletoe family and horticulturists find it difficult to raise from seed. In our garden we leave the technology to the mistletoe bird and enjoy the fruits of his labour.

The seeds of the Christmas tree had been sent to England by Georgiana Molloy, a remarkable woman who, with her husband, came out to settle at the Swan River, Western Australia in 1830. As she had grown up in Scotland, the Australian bush at first seemed to her strange and the flowers insignificant and small, but over a short lifetime her interest grew rapidly.

She received a gift of seeds from an English horticulturist Captain James Mangles, who was a cousin of Lady Stirling, wife of the Governor of Western Australia but a stranger to Georgiana. Coupled with the gift was a request for a reciprocal package of Australian seeds. This request kindled a passion in Georgiana which changed her from an amateur gardener into a true botanist.

Over the period 1836–42 Mangles received hundreds of letters and specimens from Georgiana. She once wrote: 'Fond as I ever have been of gardening, I have always avoided the tedious operation of gathering seeds.' Does that strike a chord? Not only did she gather seed from hundreds of different species of plants, some quite unknown, but she spent many evenings patiently and conscientiously packaging, labelling and numbering her specimens, even making the little paper bags in which to send them on a long and slow journey to the other side of the world.

Looking for new plants as she rambled in the bush with her little children became a favourite pastime for them all but, riding out on horseback to collect seed from previously noted plants, Georgiana was often frustrated when she found that the seed pods had opened due to a sudden burst of heat and scattered the seed. Another cause for disappointment was the depredations of birds and insects who were equally interested in the seeds.

I feel unbounded admiration for Georgiana. Not only was she a courageous pioneer, who had the usual share of tragedy in her life (including the death of her only little boy who drowned in a well), but she had the 'odious drudgery of cheese and butter making'. Teaching her children and much else besides left her little time even for her own garden.

At this time other botanists such as Ludwig Preiss were gathering hundreds of Western Australian plants for their herbariums. Preiss, who stayed for a month in Mrs Molloy's house, later published with other botanists *Plantae Preissanae*. In this book he described specimens from Mrs Molloy's collections but made no mention of her name!

Nevertheless, thanks to her largely unacknowledged work as a seedswoman of great dedication and expertise, many hitherto unknown plants were added to the collections of the world's great botanists though only one bears her name, *Melaleuca teretifolia* 'Georgiana Molloy', which was thought to be a cross between *M. lateritia* and *M. teretifolia*. The man who had had the greatest success in growing the seeds she had sent from Australia, wrote an accolade for Captain Molloy when she died aged only thirty-seven. 'Not one in ten thousand who go out into distant lands has done what she did for the Gardens of her Native Country.'

There is an abundance of seed awaiting us in our bush gardens and so many of the native plants and trees grow easily and quickly from seed that I feel ashamed at the weak-kneed way in which I buy ready-made plants instead of rearing them myself. Seeds from some of the varieties of acacia and other hard-coated seeds can be rubbed between sheets of sandpaper or stood in boiling water briefly before planting to ensure germination. Instead of talking about it, I must get into action. At least I don't have to make little paper bags in which to store my treasures, nor do I have to go very far to procure the seeds of our native plants, they are right here in our garden.

A tree which is partly parasitic is *Exocarpus cupressiformis*, commonly called wild cherry. This name refers to the ripe fruits which in winter and spring are hard green ovals on the ends of swollen fleshy red stalks which resemble the cherry. This attractive tree reaches 10 metres in height and is found scattered amongst other trees in our area, especially among she-oaks. I break one of the ten commandments regularly when I observe with covetous eyes these plants springing up joyfully in my neighbour's garden, only feet away from my barren ground. Well—he deserves them and my ground is not really barren. Perhaps when I cease to covet, one will spring up amongst my trees.

Pathways 7

Bird pool.

WHEN WALKING IN THE BUSH WHERE THERE ARE NO MARKED tracks, our eyes and feet tend instinctively to dictate the path we tread. Usually we take a slightly meandering course, rounding a clump of grass here, a tree trunk there. Following the tracks of wallabies and wombats sometimes brings us up short, where their lack of height has allowed them to bound down dense tunnels of bush. But the principle is the same. Making paths in one's bush garden is a matter of trial and error, but once plants and trees start to grow, so do the paths.

In the beginning, we cut a swathe through the rough sword grass, the blades of the motor mower set very low. On this we tramped up and down and then covered it with a litter of bark, leaves, she-oak needles and seed pods to give a soft and natural appearance. A path which winds in and out between trees tends to lead one on in anticipation of the unexpected. A pond at the end of the path is a focus for the garden, with a backdrop of trees to set it off. Medium-sized rocks, half-buried and placed here and there in haphazard fashion beside a pathway, help to outline it without making it look formal or contrived. A path leading to a rustic seat, set with its back into a screen of trees or bushes, gives one a pleasant spot to rest from one's labours, or merely to sit and contemplate life in the garden. Perhaps it would be a good thing if we took more time to observe the simple beauties of our environment. There is a lot to be seen and it is all absolutely free.

As our block is on a rise, the front paths go downhill, while the back garden is on an upward slope. The downward sweep leads the eye on and creates an illusion of distance, whereas looking uphill has a foreshortening effect. The view is immediate.

Cutting two paths into the bank at the back of the house was a different proposition from the front. Not only was it steeper but, due to drainage of water both from our garden and from blocks behind us, it was wetter. As we had some handmade bricks left over from the building, we constructed a low curving retaining wall along the base of the bank; then planted the bank with melaleucas, prostrate and other grevilleas, *Correa alba*, *C. reflexa*, maidenhair and the summer flowering *Jasminum officinale*, which is a vigorous twiner reaching 6 to 9 metres. It is not a native climber, but its delectably sweet-smelling white, starry flowers bloom over a long summer season to autumn.

Steps for the paths were made from the old bricks and very quickly the melaleucas planted beside the paths grew and suckered. After one spectacular fall down the steps, which winded one of us completely, we decided to instal a rustic handrail. Built from tea-tree, it blends well both with the paperbark and other tea-trees which have since been planted. Although it is not a large and sturdy rail, it provides the sort of fingertip control which is all that is required. Several terracotta dishes of water have been placed in amongst the shrubs, one sitting on top of a disused terracotta pipe. From the bedroom windows one gets an un-impeded view of the activities of the birds as they enjoy their baths.

Soon after we came to live in this area, we heard at night-time a curiously sweet ringing sound like little bells in the sky. Some naturalists know the sound of this little ventriloquist and many have tried to find its source. Our youngest son was determined to

Trunks of casuarina.

Hakea laurina.

identify the creature and one night, crawling round the bank with a torch, he found a small, locust-like insect which he captured in a jar. Filling the jar with leaves, he set off next morning on his way to school to visit the naturalist Graham Pizzey. At first the response was negative, but at the psychological moment our hero raised its wings and lo! emitted its tinkerbell sound. We have a special affection for this small creature for it starts to ring its bell at approximately the same time every year. Within five to seven days on either side of our son's birthday in February, this little harbinger of the bell-ringing season starts up. In twenty years it has never failed to keep its appointment with its admirers. The National Museum in Melbourne knows it only by the generic name *Eugryllodes*, meaning 'beautiful cricket'. For all we know, our peeper may not yet have been given a specific name.

As with the front garden, our feet dictated the path we took up the back. Nothing in the natural world grows in straight lines, or in geometric shaped beds. Hence, paths do best to meander amongst clumps of trees, occasional rocks, tussocks of grass and thickets of shrubs. One small track leads off to a pond overhung by an *Allocasuarina verticillata* and an *Acacia pycnantha* (golden wattle). It is circled by several slender-trunked melaleucas and an *Acacia longifolia* which we prune to keep it slight. At the foot of the casuarina grows a staghorn fern on a log of wood. Out of a dead tree fern trunk grows a clump of the *Kingianum* orchid which sends up sprays of small mauve flowers in late spring. In a pot placed in the shallow end of the pond and disguised by rocks is a delicate-looking but sturdy plant named *Villarsia parnassifolia* which has leaves rather similar to a violet. On its long stems it bears simple, attractive, five-petalled yellow flowers and thrives either in damp soil or in a container in shallow water. It blooms through spring and summer to autumn. Maidenhair fern and the small carrot fern adorn the bank and the pool is patronised by the south-eastern rosella. Very often I find a single discarded blue and green feather by the water so, even when I don't see it, I know it has been visiting. Nearby under the trees is a comfortable wooden bench for observing life at the pond.

Another track branches off and wanders up the back of the block to a rustic but sturdy wooden workshop. Constructed of old slabs of solid wood with small French doors complete with brass handles, it is laid on a concrete base. This workshop cum toolshed blends in happily with its bush surroundings. In front of the very large window, we planted a *Eucalyptus caesia*, that striking medium-sized tree which has a powdery white trunk and exquisite rosy pink flowers with yellow anthers. Apart from its beauty, it is a great bird attractor and flowers in winter and spring. It likes full sun and plenty of water and grows in medium to heavy soil. As its roots take a while to get a good grip on life, it is advisable to anchor the tree with one or more heavy rocks placed over the root area. Staking young trees is not always advisable; far better to build a small protective shelter around them until they are well established. If, however, staking is regarded as necessary, avoid at all times lashing the tree tightly to the stake like a splinted limb.

By placing two stakes, one on each side of the tree, and tying them with a figure of eight to the tree, it has room to move within the tie and cannot be damaged. Like other trees—the exotic silver birch springs to mind—these eucalypts look particularly charming planted in a group of three or more.

A *Hakea laurina* (pincushion tree), a *Callistemon citrinus* and the blue-flowered *Alyogyne huegelii* were also planted outside the window of the workshop. The hakea has grown into a tall weeping tree with long trails of foliage hanging down like curtains. The cream and red pincushion flowers make a striking display and are very attractive to the birds. The callistemon has a brief but brilliant display of red flowers in the spring when it is subject to an onslaught from the less than gentle wattle bird, whose desire for nectar outruns his good manners. *Alyogyne huegelii* is a shrub I highly recommend. Its delicate looking large clear blue flowers are similar to the hibiscus and are produced throughout the year. Picked in bud, they look charming in a vase of native flowers.

At the back of the shed, a faint path wanders through the grass to the vegetable patch which has latterly become somewhat neglected. A lemon, a grapefruit, a peach and a nectarine tree grow healthily amongst the grass despite the neglect and provide an occasional bounty. Beating the possums to the harvest is something I haven't really mastered, although bagging the peaches sometimes has them tricked.

Such are our pathways, leading one on, not with a sense of urgency, but with a gentle insistence that there is something ahead to enjoy.

8 Clothing the Nakedness

Pandorea jasminoides.

IN MOST GARDENS CUSTOM, NEIGHBOURS OR NECESSITY dictate the need for fences. These can be unsightly and, in a bush garden, destroy the illusion of being in the bush. However much one wishes to obey the command 'to love thy neighbour as thyself' there are times when privacy is valuable and an uninterrupted view of an other's activities can inhibit the pleasure we get from our gardens. Sheds also can be an eyesore, but creepers, climbers, twiners and crawlers, combined with a well thought-out screen of trees and shrubs, can disguise the presence of these necessary evils.

We are fortunate to have neighbours who have not felt it necessary to erect fences on the sides of their front gardens, so we have a continuous stretch of bush along four blocks of land. This, I am sure, has contributed greatly to the large number of birds we get in our garden and is something that could be emulated in town gardens. There is, of course, the problem of pets, but a back garden can always be fenced off, leaving the front untrammelled. Nevertheless, even if fences have to be erected, all is not lost. Neither is it total disaster if the next-door property is, in your eyes, a less than thrilling sight. It is a challenge that can be met by skilful planting.

There are several ways of getting round the ugliness of fences. If your neighbour doesn't mind the planting of medium-sized trees, but wants a fence as well, then wire mesh is sufficient to contain dogs and can quickly be covered with creepers, or screened with shrubs of varying heights. If there is room on the land, a boundary of trees planted in an irregular line and merging into shrubs of diminishing height can quickly become one with a bush garden.

Care needs to be taken, particularly in small suburban blocks, not to plant a tree on your boundary that is going to attain a massive height. Such a tree can cause problems by casting too much shade on your neighbour's property, or extracting through its roots too much nourishment or moisture from the soil. Just give a little thought to your choice of tree.

For the back line of your planting, a range of quick-growing, medium-sized acacias and eucalypts, should make a good framework, with a centre line of banksias, callistemons, hakeas, melaleucas and prostantheras to fill in spaces in the fast growing back-line trunks. The front line can be filled by an endless variety of small shrubs. It is important to plant all of these at the same time so that they get away to an equal start and share of nourishment; it is difficult to establish native shrubs under well established trees. If you make your choice of planting from guaranteed quick-growing varieties, the fence, visually, will soon be a thing of the past.

Another form of fence, which is in keeping with a bush garden, is a 2-metre tea-tree or melaleuca fence. The latter is usually constructed from freshly cut *Melaleuca ericifolia* (swamp melaleuca) and the green brush smells delectable. One could wish the colour would linger, but it browns off in time, though still looking in keeping with a bush garden. It makes a splendid frame for light, native creepers and in no time you can cover it with such runaway delights as *Pandorea pandorana*, which travels at high speed. In my neighbourhood it has spread through a row of quite unexceptional trees. Climbing through them to a height of about 8 metres and spreading outwards to the same distance, its masses of creamy flowers provide a dramatic contrast to the sombre dark green of the trees through which it travels. It has transformed a dull vista into a sight beyond imagining.

Another creeper on a more modest scale is *Clematis microphylla* (small-leaved clematis) which in our garden is planted at the base of a clump of *Melaleuca ericifolia*. It has threaded its way through the branches and arched across a small pathway into the arms of a welcoming tea-tree. The star-like cream flowers on its slender stems give it a delicate air, as do the fluffy masses of seed, which in the case of its relative *Clematis aristata* give rise to the name 'old man's beard'. It is quite a tough little creeper, whose stems are much patronised by the small birds who use them as swings.

In Queensland, there is a flowering creeper named *Petrea volubilis*. It is an evergreen plant, which twines up to about 7 metres and grows in what is called a dry tropical area, where the rainfall is 1000 millimetres a year. When in bloom, it is covered with masses of sky-blue starry flowers, which hang in cascades similar to wisteria. Because the deep blue sepals remain after the flowers are finished, its beauty lasts from spring to summer. Confusingly, its common name is purple wreath. Planted in rich moist well-drained soil, it seems to be happy in semi-shade or sun. Twining its way up a tall tree or along a trellised fence, it is a sight to remember.

Other hardy and attractive climbers include the kennedias. *Kennedia nigricans* has dramatic yellow and black flowers; *K. rubicunda*, a robust native of forest and coastal heath, has large dusky crimson flowers, and both of these plants quickly cover a shed or fence. *K. beckxiana* has narrow leaves, with downward rolled edges. It is not unlike a bright red hardenbergia, to which the kennedia family is related. Our *K. beckxiana* has covered a wire fence and set off through the branches of a nearby *Acacia sophorae*, surprising one with its vivid red splashes of colour.

The hardenbergias, of which there are several varieties, are one of our most attractive climbing plants, which in late winter and spring are covered in clusters of rich violet-blue small pea flowers. I love them for their adaptability and generous supply of bright flowers over a long period.

43

Symphony in white—Tea-tree and wedding bush.

Wattle on the roadside verge.

Another hardy quick-growing creeper is *Sollya heterophylla* (bluebell creeper). It also flowers over a long period and if it can't find a fence or a tree to twine round it will twine on itself. This attractive plant has the potential to become a weed, so readily does it seed.

An unusual creeper is the native passionfruit, which bears edible fruit. *Passiflora cinnabarina*, described alluringly as the red passionflower, has typical slender twining tendrils, which quickly make their way up any support. The leaves are deeply lobed and the flowers are, in my view, a glowing Chinese red. I have eaten the fruit, which could hardly be described as an epicure's delight, but is quite innocuous and if you were dying of thirst would seem like a miracle.

Pandorea jasminoides has all the attributes of a good climber. It is very vigorous and soon its glossy green leaves cover any unsightliness. The flowers, which are tubular, come in white or pink and have a throat splashed with claret. It's a beautiful sight for months on end, from spring through to autumn and, as an added bonus, will layer. If allowed to clamber through the trees, it will hang down to form a cool bower in summer.

Hibbertia scandens is a scrambler that will travel through trees or shrubs as well as climbing up posts. It bears wide, open-faced, bright yellow flowers and is hardy. *Chorizema cordatum* is a tough, sprawling undershrub, happy in sun or part shade and is amenable to being trained up through such plants as the purple hardenbergia or small wattles with stunning effect. It bears flowers which spring alternately from the slender stem in psychedelic colours of orange and magenta, with a small touch of yellow. Each flower wears a hat of orange upswept from its magenta face.

With these creepers and many more to choose from, there is really no excuse to have any ugliness exposed to view in your garden.

No Maintenance?

Kennedia prostrata
(running postman).

THERE IS A COMMON MISCONCEPTION THAT A BUSH GARDEN requires little or no maintenance, which makes us bush gardeners smile wryly. Certainly, if you let nature take over in a totally indiscriminate fashion and enjoy watching mayhem, without raising a finger to control matters, it can be a very laid-back business, resulting in the survival of the fittest.

One of the more important rules for growing a native garden is to avoid digging and excess watering. Although hardy in many respects, native plants will die if their root systems are disturbed. Herein lies an essential difference between a formal garden and a bush garden. Where weeding and cultivating the soil around the plants is part of the routine in a garden of exotic flowers, mulching heavily with leaf litter and bark, and the placement of rocks helps the healthy survival and natural appearance of a native garden. Less disturbance of the soil means more likelihood of tiny terrestrial plants appearing, such as lilies of many varieties, grasses, orchids, irises and many other small treasures.

Ground cover is another way to suppress weeds, retain moisture and provide a natural carpet beneath the trees. *Dichondra repens*, commonly called kidney weed, is a hardy small spreading herb, which grows well in shady dry positions. It has an extensive root system, which facilitates its rapid spreading habit. Almost unseen beneath the kidney-shaped leaves are the tiny five-petalled white flowers at the leaf base. It is now used quite commonly not only as ground cover, but as a lawn substitute. It flowers from September to December.

Viola hederacea (native violet) holds up its charming purple and white flowers from a clump of six or seven leaves. Although it has no scent, this deficiency is redeemed by its long flowering period and its ability to spread very rapidly. It tends to wilt in the hot summer sun if allowed to dry out completely but otherwise will thrive year long. It is a must beside a pool or under the trees, where it naturalises quickly.

Two other small charmers are *Goodenia humilis* and *Isotoma fluviatilis* which I have seen densely covering a lawn area which gets waterlogged in wet weather. In the full sun, these two plants flower at the same time, the yellow of the goodenia merging with the heavenly blue starlike flowers of the small creeping isotoma. The bright red pea flowers of *Kennedia prostrata* (running postman) make this an attractive ground cover, as it sprawls over banks or through the grass. It seems to have a preference for clay soils, where it grows strongly. Its big brothers, *K. nigricans* and *K. rubicunda* are very vigorous climbers or crawlers which will cover a wide area very quickly. Because of their vigour, a sharp eye has to be kept on them if strangulation of innocent plants is not to occur.

Less prostrate but very vigorous ground cover plants are found amongst the wattles. The prostrate forms of *Acacia baileyana* and *A. pravissima* (golden carpet) make a stunning sight when in full flower, covering or smothering unwanted weed growth. Grevilleas come in many prostrate forms. *Grevillea repens* forms a dense ground cover and its deep red toothbrush flowers are produced from October to February. One of its strong points is the fact that it is suited to semi-shade or even full shade, which is a bonus in a bush garden where places in full sun are at a premium. *G.* 'Poorinda Royal Mantle' has covered a large area of a bank in our garden with astonishing speed. It has attractive toothed foliage and deep red toothbrush flowers. Some others that have prospered are *G. aquifolium, G. gaudichaudi* and *G. thelemanniana.*

The well-known purple and violet *Hardenbergia violacea* adds a rich note of colour to the garden. It has a long flowering season through from winter to spring. Its purple pea flowers are produced in long racemes and the plant thrives in a well-drained situation. A drive in the country in late winter will very often reveal the glorious sight of sheets of purple draping the banks of the roadside, with a backdrop of golden wattles to complete the picture.

Leaving your garden in summer time to go on a holiday is as nerve-racking as leaving your children in the care of others as you take a well earned rest. Part of you can't wait to get away, while another part fusses round making last minute inspections, tidying up, cossetting the more frail members and feeding and watering everything in sight.

Returning on New Year's Day from a five-week holiday, our garden appeared to have changed into a tropical wilderness. Where all had been semi-ordered and weeded, precious plants had completely vanished from sight. Certainly nothing was suffering from drought; quite the reverse.

Such are the vagaries of our weather that a week later fierce heat did its best to demolish the plants that had been revelling in endless rain. As luck would have it I was away again for five days and in that time tree fern fronds frizzled and browned off and several different varieties of boronia looked far from well. *Pultenaea gunnii* (golden bush pea), a plant indigenous to the area and a recent purchase, had totally collapsed and *Prostanthera lasianthos* (Christmas bush) had an ominously dead-looking branch of flowers. I can only conclude that the enormous variation in weather conditions had unsettled these precious members of our bush garden.

Unfortunately in this country of ours, which is blessed with such a wonderful variety of plants and trees, we have been cursed with the introduction of unwelcome and brash invaders, who have taken to our soil with a vengeance. Not only are they great survivors, but they outdo many native plants striving for a place in the sun.

The arum lily, whose formal beauty makes it prized both in

the garden and in floral arrangements, has broken loose and can be found choking creek beds and densely crowding the cliffs of bayside areas. Where there is ample water, as in the seepage found on cliffs and creek banks, it thrives and completely overpowers the natural plants which normally hold the soil.

Even more insidious is the prevalence of the watsonia. It is amazingly hardy and grows thickly in either wet situations or in open well-drained areas. It can be seen on the sides of the road or in parks, reserves and open forests. It has a very strong grip on life and will break off in your hand if you try to pull it out; go forth armed with a spade or fork to do battle with it. Freesias and ixias can also be found growing wild over a wide area. I admit to having difficulty maintaining any sort of rage against freesias, for their sweet perfume is disarming and they quickly die down after flowering, becoming indistinguishable from the local grasses. Nevertheless, they are usurping the rightful place of our own wildflowers and grasses.

In our bush garden we have been weeding out determined invaders from the blackberry family for thirty years. I suspect that the constant dispersal of its seed throughout the country is perpetrated by that other immigrant, the blackbird. In a bush garden which, it is said, 'requires no maintenance', I spend half my time repairing the damage wrought by that melodious and maddening bird. When I hear its song at evening, I am completely won over by its beauty but, on glancing through the window at dawn, I observe the bird methodically scratching out every scrap of mulch from round some precious plant and a red mist rises in front of my eyes. Roots are bared to the sun and moisture is quickly lost through the bird's activities and sometimes, if I am not around, death follows. I like to think it would be so much happier in England where it has no detractors.

Two of the most intractable invaders come from South Africa where the climate is temperate and similar to our own. Boneseed and polygala have become a plague in some parts of Australia and boneseed is causing considerable erosion on cliff faces, mountain sides and creeks. It is easily pulled out as the roots are not very big, but it is a constant battle to keep it from returning. Turn your back for a year and the garden would be full of it. The sad thing is that many people don't as yet know it is a weed and are heard admiring its charming yellow daisy flower.

Running postman.

Dead tree with mistletoe.

It seems strange to call a native plant a weed, but such is the case with *Pittosporum undulatum*. This glossy leaved and hardy tree, commonly found in moist gullies, is now proliferating, the seed spread by the blackbirds. Because of its delightful perfumed flowers and attractive clusters of orange berries, it is a popular garden tree, but the seedlings should be pulled out wherever they are found.

Sollya heterophylla, that charming bluebell-flowered creeper or scrambler, is another plant in our garden which seeds very easily and is escaping into the bush. Because it is very hardy, there is a danger that it may oust less robust but indigenous plants from their own area. Once again, one must be firm about pulling out the excess seedlings.

One of the sad things about trying to retain bushland is the inevitable collision between so-called progress and the desire to retain the status quo. The sealing of roads, it has to be said, is easier on the shock absorbers of our cars, but the downside is that most people tend to drive much faster on our hitherto quiet roads, making it hazardous for humans and animals who have been in the habit of going for a gentle stroll. The process of sealing roads and installing drainage plays havoc with the road verges, very often the harbour of native grasses and wildflowers. Worse than this, however, is the introduction, via the wheels of machinery, of many noxious weeds. Our hitherto comparatively weed free verge now sports an uncommonly healthy mat of capeweed, dandelions, paspalum and couch grass. To be fair, a small patch of blackberry was there previously and has resurrected itself after being buried deep in clay and muck—a testament to its vigour.

In some places I have observed with dread the presence of oxalis, which should be dug out meticulously by hand at first sighting. I need ten pairs of hands and the patience of Job. To get rid of this invasion of unwanted pests without recourse to sprays, requires a strong arm and back, not to say large amounts of patience. Muttering imprecations directed at progress and the follies of our predecessors who brought these plants to our land helps a little to ease the aches and pains consequent upon the necessary weeding.

On the positive side, though, on our devastated verge, a few native plants have valiantly struggled through. One small

Goodenia geniculata has appeared, several *Acacia paradoxa* and *A. pycnantha* and one precious *Kennedia prostrata*. Other indigenous seedlings to emerge are those of the *Allocasuarina verticillata*. This is of particular importance as the older casuarinas in the garden are beginning to die off, leaving a wide space in the upper storey. Some of the seedlings will be transplanted with great care to another spot in the garden, always making sure that a large square of soil is lifted with the seedling so as not to disturb the small roots.

As is so often the case in a bush garden, some things die of old age, but the disappointment is softened by the regeneration of other native plants. Having scattered on the decimated garden verge handfuls of seed both of *Themeda triandra* (kangaroo grass) and *Leptospermum continentale*, the small prickly tea-tree, we were delighted to discover small seedlings of tea-tree pushing up through the poor soil. They grow easily from seed and, although common in the area, we had none in our garden, other than several we had planted. By painstaking weeding and staking out the claims of these small regenerating plants, we may yet restore to a natural state a very unnatural invasion of introduced weeds and poor topsoil.

Another aspect of maintenance in a bush garden is dealing with the decay and death of large trees. Suddenly and without warning a large tree can be uprooted in a high wind, its root system having become waterlogged through heavy rain. The fall of such a tree can cause considerable dismay at first, but after clearing up the mess and sawing up the branches, which replenish the supply of firewood, very often one finds the unusual space in the garden opens up new possibilities and new vistas.

We tend to leave a few dying trees in the garden, as the birds greatly favour them as perches for sunning and preening themselves and insects and grubs make their home in the bark and wood. Gradually, time and the weather have their way and bit by bit the dead wood drops off, causing little damage. If we had decided to have them cut down, we saw a risk, as even with the best will in the world, it is hard for someone using a chainsaw not to inflict damage in a thickly wooded bush garden, quite apart from the nervous tension such an operation produces in the onlooker.

10   *Bracken, Ferns and Ancient Life Forms*

Blue wrens in marital harmony.

AVING GROWN UP IN AN ERA WHEN FARMERS WERE heard to curse the bracken which grew so vigorously on their precious land, we took some time to appreciate its beauty. On our first block there was a great covering of bracken and we methodically and earnestly pulled it out, thinking that by so doing other plants would regenerate. Only later did we discover that many of the local wildflowers grew best amongst the bracken. It is said that there are nodes of nitrogen in the roots of bracken which nourish the soil. Apart from this, we came to realise not only how right it looks in a bush garden, but how the little birds love it. Blue wrens, one of our favourite little birds, swing on the stems and tuck their nests amongst the fronds, secure from predatory eyes. In winter the fronds turn purple, but in the spring fresh green fronds unfurl like young tree ferns. As the fronds die, they turn copper and grey, making a handsome

frame for flower arrangements, either fresh or dried. One could
call it the poor man's fern.

Having so carefully removed the bracken we then had to set
about returning it to the garden. As we have many large trees
now which cast shade, the bracken does not run wild but adds its
contribution to the natural view.

In Australia there are still pockets of remnant rainforest, which
support a range of ferns, sub-tropical trees and plants which grow
abundantly in the rich mulch of generations of trees and plants.
We should fight to the death to save these miraculous examples
of nature's diversity and wonder. The rainforests of the world
still contain thousands of life forms, some of which have yet to
be identified, others containing the possibility of life-giving and
life-saving properties, yet to be researched.

There are about 350 species of Australian ferns, found mostly
in the moist gullies of south-eastern Australia and in the rainforests of the north. They are amongst the earliest plants known
to man and we need to learn from nature how to plant them.
Depending on how you plant them in your garden, they can look
absolutely right or absolutely terrible. Ferns, trees, rocks and
water seem inextricably tied together. If we are not fortunate
enough to have a creek running through our garden, we can still
have the serenity of water in a pond. As ferns do best in dappled
to full shade, we need a large tree or clump of trees under which
to plant them. They luxuriate in cool moist places free from frost
and wind and even where there is no surface water they will
colonise rotting logs and creep over moist stone. *Asplenium
flabellifolium* (necklace fern) is the sweetest little plant which
asks to be hung round the soft neck of a child. It trails over logs
and rocks in damp places. Sometimes, from the end of a frond, a
new little plant develops as is also the case with *A. bulbiferum*,
commonly called hen and chicken fern. *Cheilanthes tenuifolia*
(little rock fern) is remarkably hardy and is found growing in the
mountains, by the coast, and even in the open country where the
rainfall is low. The ferns which do need water in our garden are
Blechnum nudum (fishbone fern), *B. wattsii* and *Gleichenia
microphylla* (coral fern). The latter is a stunning sight to see in
the bush where it grows rampantly on creek banks or where there
is permanent moisture. It foams with delicate masses of coral-like
leaves attached to thin spines and forms wonderful thickets for

little birds. Sadly, our splendid clump died after some years; the position it was in did not stay consistently wet and a short period of neglect was enough to dishearten it. Even a very small bush garden can have a little rainforest, but care must be taken not to let the ferns dry out, or they will frizzle and dry off.

The beautiful tree fern, *Dicksonia antarctica*, sheds a radiance over the ferns beneath it as it soars with majestic grace to a great height. Although the fronds grow quickly, the trunk is slow growing and makes a good host for other small ferns and epiphytic orchids, such as the orchid *Dendrobium kingianum*. Sadly sometimes, one sees these dwellers of the moist forest gullies planted in a straight line along a path leading to such a visual horror as the rotary clothes line. As with everything we plant in the bush garden, we need to try to create a sympathetic environment suited to the needs of the plants.

Xanthorrhoea australis, commonly called the grass tree, is another ancient form of life still to be found in all states of Australia except Queensland and Western Australia. If you are lucky enough to have them on your land, treasure them, for they can be a focal point of your landscape. Otherwise you have three options. You can buy one of reasonable size at vast expense from a specialist nursery, or you can plant for posterity by buying a very small plant with just a few leaves. They are very, very slow growers so you must think in terms of your great-grandchildren reaping the benefit of your vision. The third option, a sad one, is to do without a grass tree.

The small grass tree, *X. minor*, unlike *X. australis* is trunkless, with a subterranean butt. The grass-like leaves are long, pointed and rigid, so mind your eye when bending over them. They arise from the ground in a dense tuft and the single cylindrical flower spike rises to a height of 1 metre, bearing many creamy white and brown flowers whose nectar is irresistible to the birds and the bees. We have three of these small grass trees growing naturally in our garden and, although they have not yet flowered, I treasure them.

To see either of these grass trees growing in the wild is to feel strongly the antiquity of our land. With age, the trunks of *X. australis* become bent, assuming amazing shapes with arthritic looking knobs and swellings. The spreading skirts of the leaves old and new give them a majestic dignity and their ability to

Xanthorrhoea minor—the small grass tree.

Xanthorrhoea australis.

The lush beauty of ferns.

survive fire and drought have made them great survivors from earlier times.

One other ancient form of plant life we have in our bush garden is a very small cycad, *Macrozamia*, known as burrawang. Cycads, described as living fossils, were flourishing in the far distant days when birds had teeth. Can one imagine a modern day magpie solemnly chewing up its food like a well brought up child? Alas! with the loss of teeth came the loss of good manners. There are only a few dozen species of cycads left in warmer areas of the world. In Queensland and New South Wales macrozamias grow lustily, their palm-like fronds fanning out gracefully from the base of the plant. They bear large cones shaped like pineapples, which carry vivid red seeds. Clearly we can't all have these ancient treasures, but maybe our 10 centimetre high specimen will be given a lease of life for the next two or three generations. They live for maybe a thousand years, so it is exciting to think you may be nurturing a living fossil.

A Touch of Blue 11

Wahlenbergia communis, our Australian bluebell.

MOST OF US WHEN PRESSED ADMIT TO A FAVOURITE colour and, without hesitation, I say that mine is blue. I have a passion for every shade of blue, from palest azure, turquoise and sky blue, to deep cobalt. If I lived in another age and another situation in life, I would wish to be hung about with wonderful gems: sapphires from pale to deepest blue, aquamarines and zircons like the still, clear waters of the shallow sea and turquoises that almost feel blue and are seen in so much of the ancient jewellery. Well, I don't think I shall be decked out in blue jewels in this lifetime, but they are everywhere in our bush.

In our bush garden, many blue wildflowers appear each spring. Although I get great pleasure from watching the things that we have planted grow and bloom, I feel especially thrilled when flowers pop up of their own accord. To see native grasslands and grassy woodlands covered in wildflowers gives one a feeling of childlike amazement. I shall never forget driving along the Victoria Valley road in the Grampians and being brought up short by the sight of a whole paddock covered in a sheet of blue *Brunonia australis*, commonly called the blue pincushion. It has a combination of bright blue flower heads and silky leaves, which make the species unmistakable, and here they were in such abundance that one could not walk in the paddock for fear of squashing them underfoot. It is widespread in woodland and dry forest throughout Victoria and grows in what little area is left untouched in my region. A small patch in our garden has re-emerged each year, but has ceased to flower.

Thelmytra aristata (scented sun orchid) makes a regular appearance in the garden. I could not say that they grow in masses, rather more truthfully, there would be five or six plants flowering each year, but that to me is more exciting than having a profusion. They have few to many vivid blue flowers which open only in sunlight and have a fleshy channelled basal leaf. This orchid once occurred abundantly in grassland areas, but is now rare and so even more precious.

The greatest joy in a bush garden is to find wildflowers reappearing after many years of absence. This week I found a treasure which I had never expected to see in our garden, as it has been wiped out from all the neighbouring environment. The startling sky-blue little pea flowers of *Comesperma volubile* (love creeper) looked up at me from a litter of gum leaves and small native grasses as I wandered, head down, through the trees. I was checking the buds on the sun orchids, as it is hard to catch them when they open. Heat brings them out but for only a short time. Other blue wildflowers out at this time are the small blue stars, the blue grass lily and the fragile stemmed bluebell with its pure, vivid colour.

Our bluebells are a constant source of pleasure to me. They are very different from those sturdy abundant English bluebells which carpet the woods in spring. Although related to the bluebells of Scotland, they appear delicate to the point of fragility as they push up through harsh soil and metal on country roadsides, bravely holding up their startling blue flowers on the slimmest of stems. The species which pops up in the distinctly harsh environment of our gravel drive, as well as other parts of the

Blue love creeper.

Bluebells in the wild.

garden, is *Wahlenbergia communis* and it is widespread in grasslands. It flowers from November to March and is remarkably hardy for such a tender looking plant.

Chamaescilla corymbosa (blue star) and *Caesia vittata* (blue grass lily) pop up in our wild garden, as do the mauve-blue flowers of *Dichopogon strictus* (chocolate lily). *Glycine clandestina*, a lovely name for the clandestine creeping habit of this small climber, whose flowers are like tiny clusters of wisteria, grows happily amongst melaleuca and ferns in our tiny mock creek area. Like the small mauve-fringed flowers of *Thysanotus patersonii* (twining fringe lily), one is apt to forget its existence until its vivid little blue flowers appear in spring.

From the iris family, *Patersonia fragilis* is found in areas nearby and thrives in our garden. Most of the fifteen to seventeen species which are endemic to Australia are restricted to Western Australia, but five species grow in Victoria and two on the Mornington Peninsula. *P. fragilis* likes a well drained situation and, with its showy parade of purple flags and narrow grey-green leaves, it looks well placed in a rocky area.

Orthrosanthus multiflorus, which has the cheery name of morning flag, is another hardy plant which has large tufts of erect grassy leaves and narrowly branched flower stems. Clear light blue flowers emerge from papery bracts and last one day, new ones appearing every morning. It likes a sandy situation and, although originally planted by me, it has now seeded all round the garden.

Dianella revoluta and *D. tasmanica*, both members of the lily family, thrive in our garden. *D. revoluta* bears small dark blue starry flowers on wiry much branched stems rising from a tussock of long narrow leaves. The berries are eye-catching, bright blue enamelled globes, which last a long time. *D. tasmanica* is a larger version of the same plant and has bright yellow stamens in the eye of the blue star.

Veronica gracilis, the slender speedwell, sends up two to several fragile blue flowers in spring. What charming common names many of the wildflowers have. Speedwell sounds like a blessing on this little plant and love creeper goes straight to my romantic heart.

Another early resident in our garden was *Solanum aviculare* (kangaroo apple). Colour, like beauty, is very much in the eye of the beholder and where I say the flowers are soft blue, the botanical text describes them as mauve. Well, I suppose it is just a matter of degree. In any case, this is an unusual plant whose dark green leaves have irregular finger-like lobes. The flowers of lavender-violet (I say blue) are 2 to 4 centimetres across and deeply cut between the five-pointed lobes. The ripe berries turn to vermilion and look as decorative as the flowers. Both the flowers and fruit occur over a long period. As our garden is better drained now than it was in the early days, kangaroo apples don't pop up in it as they used to do. They like moist situations such as the banks of streams.

There are other native blue or lilac flowered plants available at nurseries, including such tried and true friends as *Alyogyne huegelii* and the various hardenbergia species. Several of the mint bushes have truly violet flowers and make a spectacular sight in spring, whilst the beauty of *Dampiera diversifolia*, which occurs in the south-west of Western Australia, is a heart-stopper. It forms a compact ground cover, which is surmounted in the spring and summer by a vivid crown of small blue flowers. It is claimed that this depth of colour is rarely surpassed by any other blue-flowering species of plants. Although it survives in a wide range of conditions, it likes a well-drained site with some protection from the wind. It makes a good container plant and suckers readily, which contributes to its hardiness.

Members of the scaevola family, which sport blue fan-shaped flowers of varying sizes, look like open hands attached to the end of bristly stalks. There are many varieties of this blue fan flower from the coastal dunes to forests, and they are widespread over most of the states except Queensland and Western Australia.

The first time I saw a waxlip orchid was in the garden of my parents' holiday house on the coast. Under an ageing avenue of tea-tree, there appeared amongst the tea-tree litter, the blue, sometimes white flowers of *Glossodia minor*. A single flower is borne on a green or pinkish stem, 6 to 14 centimetres high, and once seen it had me hooked. Terrestrial orchids ever since have been a source of excitement and joy to me, outweighing the claims of lush tropical orchids, which are undeniably stunning but lack the gentle grace of the terrestrial orchids.

A lover of the Grampians' dry and sandy soil is the exquisite *Calectasia cyanea* (blue tinsel lily). To see this plant in full flower is a sight to remain in one's memory. The whole of the leafy plant is dotted with papery blue iridescent stars, which have the stiff texture of an everlasting. A plant of this grew very happily in our coastal garden, until an over-zealous helper pulled it out, mistaking it for a weed.

One other beauty is *Leschenaultia biloba*. This very small shrub has spectacular blue flowers which are produced during July to December. If you have trouble growing them in your garden, you'll find they make good container plants in combination with other small-flowering native plants such as *Correa pulchella, Epacris longiflora*, small everlastings such as *Helipterum roseum* which is an annual, and *H. manglesii*. The advantage of death (if you can call it that) in a container is that it is a simple matter to quickly replace the body. If, like me, you fall inevitably for instant effect, two or three small plants purchased in full flower bring immediate comfort to the bereaved.

There are many, many more blue flowers, including the common hovea and the swamp-loving pratia and isotoma. Look out for these when you go out into the wild places of our land, the touch of blue they bring to the landscape is a joy to behold.

The Lure of Water in the Garden 12

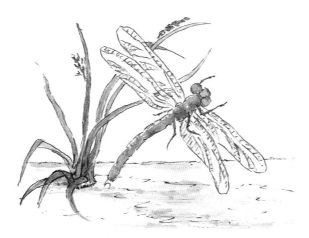

A dragonfly, fastest flier
in the insect world.

AFTER A NIGHT OF POURING RAIN, I LOOK OUT IN THE EARLY
morning upon a sun-washed garden. It is ablaze with gems.
In the *Acacia iteaphylla*, topaz, diamond and aquamarine
drops glimmer as they hang tremulous from the dangling blue-
grey seed pods. The beauty consequent upon rain led me to
thinking about water in the garden.

Water is a most precious element in our lives and we treat it
with appalling disregard. We waste it, contaminate it, drain it
away and ignore the possibilities it holds for bringing life and
loveliness into our environment. No garden, however tiny, should
be without a pool or a series of birdbaths.

There is no question that water brings birds into a garden and
it is at this point that we have to think carefully about their
natural predators, such as cats, who are ever on the lookout for a
hapless bird, made too trusting by the easy availability of a dish

of water. No container should be placed on the ground, but preferably on a bird table close to shrubs, where the birds can dart in and out. Although we humans shudder at the thought of a cold plunge in winter, birds seem to rejoice in a quick splash throughout the year.

If a tree in your garden has to be cut down, prevail upon the axeman or, to be more up to date, chainsaw man to spare the stump. Leave it at a height of about 100 centimetres, nail a sturdy piece of wood at the top of it, place a terracotta dish of water on it and, hey presto! you have a birdbath. Next, plant a creeper or clump of reeds at the base and native shrubs close by to provide shelter and a safe haven for birds, who come either to drink or disport themselves in their swimming pool. It is a good idea to put a small rock or a few stones in the dish to give them a safe foothold.

To place such bird tables outside the windows of commonly used rooms is to guarantee you hours of pleasure watching the birds as you work, eat, or sit dreaming. It is an ongoing pleasure for, just occasionally, some newcomer arrives whom you have never seen in your garden before. Such is the stuff of bush gardens. If you use your imagination, many containers can be drummed into service as birdbaths. The black lid of a long vanished rubbish bin, an old iron frying pan or battered old kitchen dishes, all look at home filled with water and stones, then placed on a moss, bark or leaf-strewn base.

One morning, as I stood at the kitchen window slicing lemon for my cup of tea, a show-off came to our garden. The question I ponder is whether he was hoping to impress a female friend. He and his mates flew in and touched down in the *Melaleuca ericifolia* which overhangs a little terracotta pool. It is frequented by red-browed finches, who range themselves along the rim beside three small terracotta birds. This day, however, it was the turn of brown thornbills and grey fantails. First the thornbills came, dipping and darting over the pool. Then came the fantails, sideslipping and glancing, their beaks and wingtips just touching the water, their fans flirting as they flew. During a slight pause in the activity, a small body suddenly launched itself from the creeper directly above the pool and landed with a tremendous thwack in the water, sending up a shower of spray. There was a moment of stunned surprise among the audience as the thornbill flew rather shakily back onto his perch. Twice more he repeated his daredevil act and then, as suddenly as they had arrived, he and his friends wheeled as one and flew off into the bright morning leaving me with a smile that lingered.

A bigger job, but one which becomes an absorbing project, is the construction of a pool. Now there are many books that tell you how to make a work of art using concrete, cement, fibreglass and such materials. In our bush garden, we tend to work rather simply and, after several grievous disappointments with cementing and fibre-glassing, we settled for a pool made from plastic, being both cheaper and simpler to manage.

Selecting a suitable site for a pool is most important, whether it be a tiny little drop-in centre for small birds or a large pond that will attract herons, magpies, parrots and other large fry. If there is a natural depression on your land, this is an obvious place to put the pool, but there are other considerations. Do you want to be able to see the pool from the house, or do you want to come upon it, as if by chance, as you wander through your bush garden, following a gently indicated track through the trees? To my mind, a pool placed under the trees looks more natural in a bush garden than one which is out in the open. Native ferns, grasses, violets, lilies and reeds grow happily in dappled shade, but struggle in the full glare of the sun. Well, having settled on the right spot, the fun begins.

As with most things in nature, pools do not come in perfect kidney shapes, circles or squares, so the digging of your pool can be quite haphazard and the shape a matter of what pleases the eye. For most bush gardens (not many of us can run to lakes) a pool does not need to be deep. Birds, insects, echidnas (if you are lucky enough to have them) and frogs enjoy a shallow pool, with a wading end where the birds can test the water as they drink. There is nothing more delightful than watching magpies or eastern rosellas at their ablutions. They flounder around in the water, dunking every part of their bodies. Eventually, when they are absolutely waterlogged, they stagger drunkenly out of the water to preen themselves and restore some sort of order to their feathers.

To end up with a depth of 18 centimetres, you need to dig a hole about the same depth again and 18 centimetres wider to allow for the rock work. Having finished the hard part of the job, that is the digging, the rest is pure pleasure. To line the pool you need heavy duty black plastic, doubled for extra strength. Lay this in the pool, bringing the sides of the plastic well up and over the top of the hole, making a ledge in the soil on which to spread the plastic. This ledge provides a firm base on which to anchor and conceal the plastic by covering it with soil, stones and rocks. Care must be taken at all points of this construction not to pierce the plastic. I don my gumboots which are great for both the initial dirty work and for standing in the water titivating the rock work. At this point, pour water into the pool to weigh down the plastic and enable you to spread it evenly, smoothing out any large wrinkles and settling it firmly into shape.

Collecting rocks for lining the pool is an intriguing pursuit. If you are lucky enough to have a friend whose land is strewn with rocks, you may be able to beg some for your project. Gone are the days when it is possible to collect them from the roadside. However, large nurseries usually stock supplies of rock, river stones and scoria, all of which are useful in the making of a pool. Jagged rocks with sharp points can present a danger if accidentally dropped on the plastic, undoing with one fell swoop the work of hours, or worse piercing the plastic without you realising it. Imagine the moment when the pool is finished, you have filled it with water and joy is unconfined. Horror strikes, when an hour or so later the water level is seen to be going down. You tell yourself, with bright optimism, that the soil is just soaking up some of the water, or that the small plants are taking in a large drink — you can't fool yourself for long. It has sprung a leak and all has to be done again. So, use flattish rocks for the base and line the sides with irregular shaped rocks fitted together so that they hold firm. Make sure that the rocks on the ledge around the pool slightly overhang the plastic so that when the pool is filled with water no plastic is visible. Sprinkle river stones and scoria in the crevices and on the bottom of the pool and then start planting.

You have various options for using the soil that you have dug out. It can be kept as a bank all around the pool, or a bank on the farthest side of the pool only. It can be carted away for use elsewhere in the garden, perhaps to make an artificial mound.

In nature's garden, a pool is rarely surrounded by brightly coloured flowers. Soft, green ferns, grasses and small plants are

Pond in Nanette Cuming's garden.

the perfect foil for the water. To strive for this natural look, we can do away with expensive or exotic plants. The green-tipped pink or red bells of *Correa reflexa*, the small mauve flowers of *Bauera rubioides*, clumps of native reeds and little rock-hugging ferns will soon transform your pool. Behind the bank, a thicket of shrubs for the birds and a few taller trees can be planted, choosing from acacias, banksias, eucalypts and melaleucas, the choice is endless.

On the low side of the pool, tuck maidenhair into a pocket of soil in the crevices between the rocks; in no time it will naturalise, softening the contours of the pool. *Viola hederacea* is another runaway delight beside water. It sends out runners and takes root rapidly, holding up its little purple and white flowers to be admired throughout the year. We planted clumps of the blue-flowering *Orthrosanthos multiflorus* beside one pond. The strap-like leaves are ornamental and the sky-blue flowers on tall slender stems are distinctive. Another bonus is its tendency to seed round the garden.

The whole area round the pool needs to be littered with dead leaves, bits of bark and, if you can get them, several big rocks, half buried in the ground like budding mushrooms. A flat rock overhanging the water makes a dark retreat for water insects and a diving board for the more adventurous small birds. In summer, dragonflies appear. These are the fastest fliers of the insect world and they look both purposeful and erratic as they zigzag across the water in search of fulfilment in their few short days of life. Damsel flies and butterflies add decorative touches as they flit above the water and frogs trill their joyful chorus.

It must be kept in mind throughout the whole enterprise, that this pool is to look natural and uncontrived, to be a source of pleasure to the living creatures who frequent it and a tranquil spot for humans. A contemplation seat is easily made from two sturdy posts sunk into the ground and a crossbar made from a thick plank. Placed under the dappled shade of a nearby tree, it is a good place from which to observe the birds. When you look into the pool, you will see reflections of the trees, sky, clouds and the moon at night — what enchantment! and all for the price of a day's labour and some heavy-duty plastic.

We experienced a moment of joyous fulfilment shortly after we had completed our first pool. Flying in over the garden came a white-faced heron who landed on the rim of the pool. Wading about, he stirred up the water, probing for bugs with his sharp bill. He became a regular visitor until the trees grew tall and obscured the pool from the air.

One other way to introduce water into the garden is by using run-off rain. Gardeners, like home decorators, often gain ideas from other people and whether they incorporate these ideas unaltered, or whether they adapt them slightly to suit their conditions, it is always a source of pleasure to improve on a garden design.

The amount of rainwater that gets flushed away down our drains from the rooftops seems a sad waste of a precious resource. One way to conserve at least some of it, is to instal a rainwater tank. In our garden, the overflow from a little tank has been taken underground for a short distance in a pipe, then surfaces as a small creek which flows every now and then after rain. Planted alongside this little watercourse are *Adiantum aethiopicum* (the maidenhair fern), which has spread thickly; larger ferns such as *Dicksonia antarctica*, the beautiful tree fern; false bracken fern; *Blechnum wattsii* (ripple fern); and various types of sedges and rushes. These all thrive in the moist ground under the shade of large she-oaks. The idea was to carry on the creek to a small pond, a good thought but, in actual fact, the water never reaches the pond, as it gets soaked up by the ferns and the roots of the trees and shrubs.

Another idea, which may not appeal to the houseproud, but which is a spectacular success in a friend's garden, came about more by accident than design, as so often happens. As the spouting on one section of the overhanging roof rotted away, the water dripped through onto tree ferns planted below. The ferns grew mightily so, instead of replacing the spouting, it was removed. Now the water from the overhanging roof nurtures a flourishing garden composed of great ferns, a brilliant *Melaleuca lateritia*, commonly called robin redbreast, which constantly sports its scarlet flowers, and a healthy specimen of *Eucryphia lucida* (Tasmanian leatherwood). This is a small tree with dark green shining blunt leaves about 3 to 4 centimetres long, the edges often slightly wavy. The large flowers form at the leaf base, their pure white petals cupping the many fragile stamens tipped with red. The bees love the nectar and leatherwood honey is greatly sought after. It is a charming tree which takes about fourteen years to flower, so plant it now if you want one.

So, instead of replacing the guttering, my friend found a new use for the rain from the roof, the garden has benefited and there is no detrimental effect to the house.

A Time of Birds   13

Rufous fantail.

THERE ARE SOME MORNINGS IN OUR LIFE WHEN THE WHOLE
world seems grey. Our ears are assailed by a battery of
unpleasant news and the din of electioneering rises to fever
pitch. We humans seem to have lost sight of the beauty that is
everywhere and a simple life is no longer good enough for us. An
obsession with material things is producing a desert in our hearts
and minds.

With these rather negative thoughts in mind, I came this
morning to get the breakfast. As I approached the floor-length
windows, I was literally brought up short. There was a pageant
of light, colour and movement going on in front of my eyes.
Afraid to move, I remained motionless in an increasingly awkward
pose. My bare feet getting ever colder on the cold slate floor,
head and neck craned unnaturally, my eyes darting from side to
side, I watched with joy the bird display.

It is difficult not to anthropomorphise about birds. For the sheer fun of it, the grey fantails seem to play chasey with each other, describing wonderful arcs and looping the loop as they fly. As is so often the case in our garden, they were accompanied by brown thornbills, who darted in and out amongst the pandorea and the jasmine, occasionally joining the fantails for a drink at the small bird pools. As if this was not enough, a family of blue wrens joined the party on the grass. They bounced up and down on their thread-like legs as if testing the springs of a grassy mattress. It is hard to believe that their tiny legs are composed of the muscles, ligaments and nerves which give them such strength. They love to fly up on to the verandah beams and explore creepers and cobwebs in the hope of finding insects to eat. They dance along the beams like gymnasts at their practice, with all the aplomb of a champion.

Further into the garden, the spotted pardalote was piping, the grey thrush produced a few lines of pure song and a magpie warbled high up in the casuarina. Some time ago I saw, with the same sense of pride that one feels when someone comments favourably about one's home, that the silvereyes had elected to build a nest in the jasmine right by the kitchen window. Urgent cheeping from deep in the creeper told of its tiny occupants and mother and father silvereye were kept very busy flying in and out with suitable provender for their importunate young. I was interested to note that the grey fantails kept up a continuous flying circuit round the silvereyes' territory, not in any aggressive fashion but more in the manner of grey nannies keeping an eye on their charges to make sure that they came to no harm. Could it be that the fanning of their tails stirred up insects for the silvereyes to catch for their young? It is a nice theory, probably off the mark, but I'm sticking to it.

A visit from the rufous fantail, that most glowing of little birds, completed my joy on this particular day. It is probably the last time I shall see this bird for many months, as it leaves in early autumn for northern parts, even as far afield as New Guinea, not returning until the spring. Its metallic call sounds something like 'tst — tst — tseeyou — tst' which seems uncommonly prophetic.

During this week, as well as the aforementioned birds, there has been the continuous piping of the yellow robin, that most endearing little bird whose trusting nature makes him an easy prey for cats. He is the first bird that I hear singing in my garden just at dawn and the last to go to bed at nightfall. What a long day for such a small creature! The eastern spinebill has returned to spend many hours each day probing with its long curved beak the flowers of all the grevilleas in the garden. It is a handsome honeyeater with its striking rufous, black and white markings and slim, elegant body, but it worries me that it spends so much energy getting its food. As fast as its sips the honey, it burns up the energy produced. It is a marvel to watch as it remains seemingly suspended by its beak, while its wings whir at tremendous speed to keep it in one place.

Others I have heard in the garden have been the grey butcher-bird, the eastern rosella, doves and a crow, the last mentioned I could do without for, although he is a most handsome bird, I don't trust his malevolent blue eye. Another black mark against his credit card is his persistent and ugly cawing and the banging of his beak on our fragile windows, several of which have been cracked by his perverse attentions.

The common bronze-wing plods round the grass eating seeds, taking off at a great rate and with a loud whirring of wings if disturbed. The brush bronze-wing has ceased to visit us since we dug out the over-exuberant *Kennedia rubicunda* on whose seeds it fed. Up in the high branches of the dead wattle tree surveying the whole garden sits a fantail cuckoo, its silhouette elegant and slim against the swiftly moving silver clouds. It has a fast, downward trilling call which is repeated four or five times. It also whistles a mournful 'whoo'. Maybe, like most other species of cuckoo, it suffers a deep-seated sense of guilt and grief for dumping its eggs in another bird's nest and not raising its young. To see a pair of small, put-upon birds, such as grey fantails, hurtling backwards and forwards to their nest trying to keep up with the voracious appetite of young cuckoos is one of the marvels of nature.

One of many varieties of birds which build artistic nests is the fairy martin. For the first ten years of our life in this bush garden, our day was often enlivened by the sight of little flocks of fairy martins flying over the garden. So fearless were they that we felt they were targeting our heads as they swooped low. We discovered their beautiful pottery nests, shaped like squat bottles, which they built into the clay cliffs of the creek below us. Not having seen them for some time, we scrambled down into the deeply eroded creek and discovered that all their little nests had been smashed, clearly the work of vandals. It was a terrible sight and reinforces my belief that children need to be taught early to value and appreciate the beauty of the bush and its creatures, which are there for us all to enjoy.

Easter has gone and only the memory of it lingers, but there is much to record in a garden notebook. As we were blessed this Easter with perfect autumn weather, sitting outside in the garden was a full-time occupation. There was no question of working; all such scruples had to be firmly suppressed, the excuse being that any activity would disturb my visitors. Let me hasten to add that it was not my human visitors I was concerned about, but the birds.

Good Friday had been a dull and sombre day in the garden. There was little sun and practically no sight or sound of birds, but on Saturday sunshine lit up the garden, transforming the bush. Dappled light came through the canopy onto the gleaming leaves of gum trees, which turn sideways to the sun's rays. The glossy, deep green leaves of the *Pandorea jasminoides* set off its white and claret flowers, while the leaves of the tall *Hymenosporum flavum* looked as if they had been specially polished.

Into this sparkling scene of light and shade came the Easter parade of birds, butterflies and dragonflies. A family of blue wrens sprang up and down on their grass trampoline and vacuum-cleaned the aphis on the roses, at intervals disappearing into a thicket of dead creeper, twittering the while. As I sat on the verandah, a pair of eastern spinebills feasted on the flowers of the red sage, not 2 metres away. The nectar must be very sweet, as they flew off every now and then to drink at one of the nearby bird pools before resuming their feast. As I sat watching, a spotted pardalote whizzed past my ear and vanished into an opening at the top of the verandah post. Clearly it thought it had found a possible place to set up home. As they nest in tunnels of their own making, it was sad to hear it scratching away at the back of the opening, vainly trying to tunnel into the side of a downpipe. After a while it flew out, returning to make one more abortive attempt. Meanwhile, a whole flurry of red-browed finches had alighted at my feet to sample the grass seeds in the rough lawn. Quite suddenly, they all took off in alarm and I was at a loss to know the reason, until I saw a grey shrike thrush

A haven for birds.

threading its way quietly up a nearby bank. Clearly the finches regard the thrush with deep suspicion, although rarely have I seen an aggressive act from this melodious songbird.

This was only the beginning of a wonderful two hours of bird visitors. Two eastern shrike tits made no attempt to disguise their presence in the garden, but sent rafts of twigs and bark rattling to the ground from high up in the trees. Then they came down to sit on the rim of a bird pool, sipping and splashing alternately. They are the most striking of birds with brilliant yellow, black and white markings and an imperial black mohawk crest which is dramatic in silhouette. A male and female rufous whistler started up a duet, or should I call it a round, one on each side of the garden. As soon as one started, the other launched into the same song, half a beat behind. A pair of willie wagtails, real dandies in their black and white tailcoats, splashed in the pond and another handsome visitor, the white-eared honeyeater, moved in as well.

Magpies dropped in for their usual worm digging stint, wattle birds shrieked unmusically in the trees, while the pigeon gently cooed as it plodded amiably round the garden. To add to this, there were visits from the yellow robin, the little thornbill, the striated thornbill, the yellow-faced honeyeater, silvereyes, grey fantails and that interloper, the blackbird, who for the sake of truth has to be noted.

The combination of sun, trees and water clearly drew the birds as a magnet and gave me heartfelt joy at this Eastertide. We must be doing something right in our bush garden, to have such lovely visitors who give much joy and make no demands upon us.

Beastly Inhabitants 14

A mistletoe bird.

O NE OF THE CONSTANT PLEASURES OF A POND IS WATCHING the bird and insect life that visits it. In my sister's bush garden in the Grampians, there is a rocky pond on either side of the living room. The glass windows and doors give an uninterrupted view of the early morning ablutions of a large variety of birds. Sitting at breakfast is a slow business when every mouthful is interrupted by the sight of an interesting visitor. Suddenly a flash of blue streaks over the pond, dipping rapidly into the water as it passes. The azure kingfisher, displaying from the side a glorious vision of blue feathers, has dropped in and as quickly gone on his business elsewhere. Having briefly recovered from the excitement of his visit, the more prosaic moments of washing up the dishes are interrupted by the sight of a pair of mistletoe birds. The lovely red splash of colour on the pursuing male caught my eye first. Standing stock-still for fear of frightening him away, I become aware of the dangling tea-towel and cooling water, animation in the garden producing suspended animation in the kitchen. What a morning, and yet these are only two of the many birds to visit! The tufted honeyeater, the yellow-faced honeyeater, the yellow-winged honeyeater, the white-naped honeyeater, blue wrens, fantails, thornbills, red-browed finches and many more revel in the water daily and are a constant source of joy.

In the evening, we hear the grunting of a koala, so off we set to find him. It is easier said than done, for after an hour's search he has still not been sighted. There are many swamp gums in the garden, so he has an assured supply of the food which he enjoys.

An echidna, his spiny back looking somewhat dusty, has retired from the laborious task of digging for ants in the red soil and is taking a nap in the hot sun. He has few, if any, predators, thanks to the armoury of spikes which enfold him. He is a comical but endearing sight waddling on his way, his long nose questing for ants as he pursues his deliberate journey.

At home, as I work quietly in the garden, I watch the small brown skinks who come out from underneath the stones or rocks and sun themselves, absorbing the last real heat they will experience until the spring. As they frisk about, my eye is taken by the activity occurring in a nest of ants, not the little, gentle ones but the large, vicious bull ants. I have to be careful where I dig and weed in our garden, for if I disturb their nest there is an instant and aggressive reaction. If ever you have been bitten by a bull ant, you will not wish to run the gauntlet too often. They construct a large mound in which there are many tunnels where they lay their eggs. As they have as much right as I to live in the garden, I tend to skirt round them and regard them with considerable respect.

Very recently, scientific research into bull ants has revealed some interesting facts. The male bull ant rarely leaves the nest except to mate and leaves the house cleaning entirely to the female! She is equipped with a gland in her armpits which secretes an antiseptic liquid that is constantly spread over her body and that of her young. This secretion is made up of many chemical compounds which kill all forms of fungal infection. Once again we may be on the edge of some new and exciting discovery for the application of this knowledge.

Just as vicious, but smaller, are the black jumper ants who also frequent the garden and, as their name suggests, can leap on you unawares, causing instant panic. These are the only two dwellers in my bush garden that ever inflict pain on me.

There are many spiders, beetles, slaters, frogs, butterflies and other flying insects which are part of the ecology and perform their allotted tasks in the life of the bush garden.

One day, having observed the unexpected death of several plants, I was wandering rather disconsolately through the seeding heads of native grasses when I happened to glance up at the mistletoe growing on an *Allocasuarina stricta*. To my joy and amazement, I beheld a sight which I had never seen in the garden before. Festooning the drooping twigs of the mistletoe and gently waving in a small breeze, were thirteen most spectacular butterflies, which had very recently emerged from their toffee-coloured chrysalises. Their almost folded wings, patterned in colours of black, grey, crimson, white and bright yellow, were hung out to air for the whole day, while they clasped the split chrysalis with fragile legs, their knobbed antennae gently feeling the air.

Next morning, some were still there, some had gone and new ones had emerged. As I sat in the grass watching, agitation started up in one as yet unopened chrysalis. Shortly, a yellow head emerged and gradually worked its way out of its prison. The forewing, a small folded grey and white bundle, its yellow markings still hidden, clung to the chrysalis for about five minutes, then started to drop what appeared to be a colourful apron patterned in red, black, grey and white — the underside of the hindwing. After fifteen minutes, the crumples had gone from the wings but the butterfly still hung almost motionless in the warm sun, its wings folded up. Later I watched one fly away, the upper side of the wings being a soft grey with a black border spotted in white, a demure colouring quite different from its glorious underside.

This butterfly, the imperial white, lays its eggs in batches which vary from twenty to sixty on the leaves of a mistletoe, usually as in this case *Amyema pendula*. The larvae feed on the mistletoe, where birds and insect parasites account for some of them. Along with the visits of the exquisite little mistletoe bird, this butterfly is a good reason to retain the mistletoe in the garden.

The joy of this discovery had quickly dispelled my gloom over death in the garden and, in the delicious warmth of a perfect summer's day, the common brown butterfly, the white butterfly and a painted lady were also seen drifting amongst the trees and low over the pathways.

Magpies, whose songs are associated with country life, moonlight serenades and early morning calls, also provide us with entertainment. Every year we have watched with amusement the importunate behaviour of the young magpies who have no apparent desire to spread their wings and let go Mother's apronstrings. Often, we have thrown pieces of bread on to the grass in answer to their peevish cries, only to watch them as they continued to shriek pathetically to Mother to feed them. Bigger already than their put-upon parents, they seem loath to give up their dependent status. They are so tame that, on invitation to enter the house, they step in the door and wander about on the slate floor quite unafraid. On another occasion, the door was left open on a hot day and, to our astonishment, we discovered a blue-tongue lizard crawling across the kitchen floor. We guided him slowly to the door and he slid off to a more suitable spot.

Another uninhibited artist is the butcherbird, whose nefarious activities are hard to reconcile with his glorious Pavarotti flights of song. A friend observed a butcherbird in her garden with a baby bird in its beak, being hotly pursued by a frantic blackbird and an equally distraught wattlebird. Whose baby was it? Had one of those birds decided to support the other in a common sense of outrage, or had they failed to check on their own offspring before setting out in pursuit? In any case, no doubt the butcherbird safely wedged his meal of baby food in a forked branch to eat at his leisure.

The brush tail possum, who inhabits the enclosed hot water tank box, is causing serious problems. Apart from the noise of her nightly circuits round the tin roof, which are more amusing than troublesome, she has caused considerable disaster to the hot water box itself. By dint of forcing her way between the wooden wall of the cottage and this enclosure, she has gradually managed to tilt the whole edifice out from the wall. It now leans on its base at a perilous angle, not improved by the fact that a baby possum has been added to the menage and mother has been squeezing herself with baby on her back, into her snug, warm nest. I fear the day of eviction is drawing near and she will have to find alternative accommodation.

Blue-tongue lizard basking.

Furry caterpillar on the move.

It is a sad fact that the population of engaging ringtail possums, who used to outnumber the brushtails in our garden, has dropped alarmingly. Where once it was a common sight on a moonlit night to see them frolicking about up in the trees, I have not seen one in the last year. Is it cats or foxes, I wonder, who are causing such depredation in our marsupial population? I believe that cats are the villains and until people take the trouble to face up honestly to the toll these natural hunters are taking of our small mammals, marsupials, reptiles and birds, we will continue to lose the rightful dwellers of the bush environment. Despite the feral predators, however, our garden continues to support a variety of creatures which surprise and delight us with their presence.

A Romantic Garden   15

Flying by radar, one of our bats

IT IS A PITY THAT THE DAYS OF FORMAL PROPOSALS OF MARRIAGE are no longer with us, for we have just the sort of garden seat that lends itself to such an occasion. The iron legs were found by our son far out in the bush somewhere and, being a born scavenger, he lugged home the two heavy iron bases. After some years, Peter rebuilt the old seat and it has been in constant use ever since; not so far as I know by lovers, but it has a romantic air about it.

A bush garden at night has it all over a conventional garden, in my view. There are soft conspirational murmurs coming from the trees as the wind swishes through the skirts of the casuarinas. The gentle chirping of crickets is heard on warm nights and bats click and twitter as they flash by with their radar turned full on. As children, we used to sit huddled under the nursery table at which we did our homework, with our felt school hats pulled firmly down to our ears, while the bats swept down the staircase and clicked around the room. Likewise, at our holiday house, bathing caps were the required headgear and tennis racquets were the means used to persuade bats to return to their night world. All such occasions were accompanied by slightly dramatised shrieks, tinged with delicious terror. Old folktales of bats becoming inextricably entangled in our hair held sway in our minds.

There is something infinitely mysterious about looking up through the tracery of trunks, branches and leaves to either a star-bright sky or an expanse of tumultuous clouds racing eastward. One-third of our lives is spent oblivious to the glory of the monochromatic night sky. Night-time presents neither the danger from ultra-violet rays nor the terrors of wild beasts. How lucky we are in Australia to live in a land inhabited by gentle and unthreatening animals, yet we shun the darkness with an almost primitive fear.

Whether seen in her mature glory or in the slender crescent of her nascent state, the sight of the moon is a continuing gift to us earthbound mortals and the embodiment of romance.

Then there are the birds of the night. For two or three years a pair of tawny frogmouths took up residence in a she-oak. One year they were accompanied by a baby who sat quietly between the parent birds looking very solemn. They are one of nature's clever adaptations, being extremely well camouflaged as they sit by day on a branch of the casuarina, looking almost indistinguishable from their perch. All day they sit, opening a wary eye at intervals to check any movement in their vicinity. Shortly before nightfall, they start to fluff up their feathers, rather as we stretch our limbs before getting out of bed. Then, quite suddenly, they spread their wings and fly quietly off for the night's hunting. I love to watch them set off and sometimes, when the spirit and the flesh are willing, I get up to watch them fly back to their perch at dawn. Then they take up their statuesque pose for the rest of the day. The following year a predator killed one of the pair and we have had no further visits.

The boobook owl is heard at night with his strange, foreboding call 'Mo-poke'. Driving home, we sometimes catch, in the headlights of the car, his gliding flight down the road. This bird is widespread over the entire continent and his call is known to many generations of Australians.

My garden.

Sometimes at night I hear the call of the spur-winged plovers as they fly overhead. It is a plaintive sound but not as heart-wrenching as the call of the curlew, which resembles the piteous cry of a child. We don't have curlews on our side of the Peninsula, so I don't have to listen to their sad song. The plovers are one of those species of bird which perform a 'broken wing' act near a nest or chicks. This gallant distraction technique on the part of the parent is very touching to my mind and may help to ensure the survival of the young. One of the more charming sights I have seen on our road was a parent plover, walking briskly up the track looking neither to right nor left with a trail of chicks bobbing and bustling along behind her.

Magpies are the songsters of the moonlight, who serenade us with song in the small hours of the night. One cannot help but feel that they are singing for joy.

There is a feeling of innocence and unspoilt beauty in the garden at night, that touches a deep chord of romance in our hearts.

Scents, Sounds and Feeling   16

Bee sipping nectar.

IN THE AUSTRALIAN BUSH THERE ARE A GREAT NUMBER OF plants with perfumed foliage, an attribute which makes strolling in a bush garden a great pleasure. To pick and crush the leaves of sweet-smelling plants gives an instant reward without harming the plant. I tend to pocket the leaves, sometimes forgetting to remove them before the washing machine has its way. Some of the best of the trees that flourish in our garden are members of the Eucalypt family, those trees synonymous with the name of Australia. Breathing in the scent of their hot dry leaves in summer or the fragrance of wet bark and leaves after rain is surely one of the pleasures of a bush garden.

Eucalyptus cinerea, Argyle apple, is a small to medium-sized tree. Its leaves are opposite, broad to round and silver in colour, which makes it attractive for indoor decoration. If a leaf is pressed between finger and thumb, not only do you release the sweet eucalyptus smell, but you leave a perfect fingerprint on the leaf. While this may not be of world-shaking importance to forensic science, it does intrigue young children.

E. globulus (Tasmanian blue gum) is well known for the beauty of its blue juvenile leaves and its strong perfume. One of its charms is the sight of the powder-blue bud caps scattered on the ground below. They are like small pixie hats and are also strongly perfumed. This tree does, however, grow to a great size and is not recommended for a small block. Sometimes we coppice them to retain the lovely juvenile leaves and stunt their growth. In our enthusiasm, when we started out we planted a tiny seedling about 3 metres from the house and inevitably it grew far larger than we had expected. It had to get the chop.

E. maculata, another tree with perfumed foliage, grows straight as an arrow to a great height. If you have room in your garden, it is a rewarding tree to grow. As the name suggests, it has a spotted trunk of infinite beauty. The many coloured flaking bark peels off in summer to reveal a smooth white surface with decorative splodges of pink, grey and purple.

E. nicholli (peppermint gum) has delicious scented leaves. It is a small, graceful tree with an open crown and dark persistent fissured bark. *E. citriodora* (lemon-scented gum) has smooth white bark which, as it ages, develops stocking-like wrinkles at its joints. It is a striking and graceful gum and the scent of its leaves is a tangy lemon.

Two other gums with perfumed foliage which we grow are *E. sideroxylon* and *E. viminalis*, the former has pink flowers and is of medium height. *E. viminalis* is indigenous to the area where we live and grows to a large tree with shaggy bark. It is one of the eucalypts favoured by the koala and once, for two magical days, we had a koala visiting one in our garden. I fear that the press of human habitation makes it a faint hope that such a visit will occur again.

Amongst many other species of trees and plants which have sweet-scented foliage, one would need to mention baeckea, boronia, crowea, callistemon, eriostemon, leptospermum, melaleuca, prostanthera and a heap of others. All you need to do when buying plants at a nursery is to press a leaf between finger and thumb to release any fragrance. You will be amazed at the number of deliciously scented leaves that there are amongst our native plants.

Colour and texture of
spotted gum trunk.

Lemon-scented gum with wrinkled stockings.

Strangely, there are fewer varieties of perfumed flowers than there are of plants with perfumed foliage, but in this context one immediately thinks of the acacia family. There is one for every day of the year and then as many again. They are spread more widely over our continent than any other plant, being found in desolate areas of desert scrub as well as areas of rich soil and high rainfall. The diversity of their foliage extends from the soft feathery leaves of the tall rainforest acacia to the flattened, spatula-like leaves of the golden wattle, to needle-pointed leaves that tear and spike the unwary, to the soft, grey caressing leaves of *Acacia baileyana* and the little grey pointed trowel-like leaves of *A. podalyriifolia*.

A. iteaphylla flowers in late autumn. This green-grey leafed small tree is to be treasured, not only for its early blossom but for the charm of its seed pods. These long blue twisted pods hang twirling from the tree like children's decorations and provide an unusual and colourful sight for many months.

In this family there are small graceful shrubs, bearing trusses, pom-poms or spikes of yellow. There are prostrate carpets of gold, middle-sized trees of widely varying shapes and large trees suitable for a big bush garden.

Acacia pycnantha, which is our national emblem, is one of the few wattles that attracts birds. It has a nectar gland at the stem end of the leaf and produces a heavy flow of nectar from June to September, attracting a variety of birds to the feast. The blossoms are large, bright yellow and have a sweet perfume. It can be pruned after flowering to keep it to a suitable size for your garden. Who has not enjoyed the rapture of smelling a cluster of wattle flowers, which lifts the spirit and puts spring in our step.

While wattles are sometimes blamed unfairly for causing hay fever, it is usually the pollen of flowering grasses which is the villain.

Hymenosporum flavum (native frangipani) described as a small to medium leafy tree, grows to a height of 10 metres in our garden. It has dark green shining leaves with terminal clusters of creamy flowers which change to yellow with age and whose fragrance is a cross between a gardenia and pittosporum. It comes from the sheltered, damp forests of Queensland and New South Wales, but has proved adaptable and hardy in our bush garden.

Related to the pittosporum family, the flowers last for two or three months. It grows readily from seed but shows no tendency to become 'feral', as does its relative *Pittosporum undulatum*.

Bursaria spinosa (sweet bursaria) is another local plant which has sweet scented flowers as do two lilies: *Arthropodium minus* (the small vanilla lily), which has purple drooping flowers, and *Dichopogon strictus* (chocolate lily), whose purple flowers are held upright along branched stems which arise from grass-like leaves. This lily pops up regularly in our bush garden and flowers from October to December.

Hoya australis, a climber which we grow in a pot and to which we give very little attention, has delightful clusters of pinky-cream waxen dewy flowers with the sweetest perfume. Whatever sized garden you have, there is surely room against a sheltered east wall for one such fragrant plant. Whatever sweet-smelling trees and shrubs you choose, be sure to plant some of them near your gate, windows and doorways.

The sense of touch is in everything. Each part of a tree has a special feel, whether it be the texture of bark, or the leaves and litter which we collect for mulch. The cool smooth trunk of a eucalypt has a sensuous charm and invites a hug or, to the less demonstrative, a stroke. All these things speak to us through our hands, which are our tools in the garden. Through them we draw a sense of companionship with the earth.

For those who are fortunate to have good hearing, a blessing we take for granted, the bush garden provides a continuous concert. Apart from the many and glorious bird songs we hear, there are other more muted sounds. Today is a day of medium wind. If I close my eyes and just concentrate on listening, the sound of the wind murmuring and sighing as it rustles the skirts of the she-oaks is magical. This is one reason to grow trees! The wildness of a storm has a different effect. There is a feeling of excitement as one listens to the cracking of thunder and the lashing of branches, with the occasional snapping sound of broken limbs. It is a huge life force rushing through the garden.

At night, the musical trilling of frogs after rain is in sharp contrast to the less than musical uproar created by possums who leap from trees on to the tin roof with a tremendous thwack, after which they either pad heavily across the roof like menacing prowlers or tear along the surface as if at a race track. Such noises are quite amusing but their discourse, whether it be angry or amatory, makes to our ears a hideous din.

The humming of bees has a drowsy summer sound and the sharp shrilling of cicadas is an indicator that hot weather is with us. Sound is an intrinsic part of a bush garden, so the introduction of bird-attracting plants, trees and water to your garden is a way of ensuring the presence of music in your life.

Spring is Sprung   17

Early Nancies.

S PRING, GLORIOUS SPRING! IT FILLS THE AIR WITH WARMTH
and its explosion of growth drives me to desperation when I
look at the jobs needing to be done. It is imperative to root
out all those hateful weeds and that vulgar bright green unnatural
grass and plant afresh in empty spaces. There is nothing more
boring in a garden than lots of bare earth. Either one must fill the
space with plants, grow tussocks of grass, plant rocks (yes, plant
them), or smother it with leaf litter and bark.

Where some bush gardeners prefer to plant natives in the
autumn, we tend to start haunting nurseries in early spring. I like
to see plants in flower, even if I am only going to buy small
editions of them. Nothing gives me greater pleasure than to
return home with a large number of small plants and to spend the
day happily finding a place for them in the garden. They should
have three months to acclimatise to their new surroundings,
before any real heat comes.

Birds are very busy at this time too, settling on new territories for their nests. As I write, there is great competition going on between the large wattle birds and a less aggressive south-eastern rosella for a place at the pond. Usually the latter gives way, being of a milder disposition. I am delighted to see the rosellas in large numbers about the garden. The dazzling red, yellow, blue and green of their feathers is heart-stopping and their soft, bell-like call is sweet, quite different from the urgent semi-shriek of their flight call. To get them to nest in the garden is tricky. If you have an old tree with a hole in it, where a branch has fallen off, you may be fortunate enough to have them move in. You can try to lure them by wiring a hollow log up in a tree. The end of the log must be blocked so that it makes a snug apartment. Very often a possum will move in with alacrity before the parrot takes the big decision to make it his home — 'the biggest commitment one will ever make'!

Within a few days of erecting a hollow log in the big old manna gum we had several interested viewers. First came the kookaburra who stood warily on the threshold, his tail quivering, either with anticipatory excitement or perhaps more prosaically to maintain his balance. We urged him on, but after several exploratory visits he left the site.

Then came a pair of rosellas. This was a big moment for which we had planned. One disappeared inside the log, whilst the other kept guard. We held our breath for a whole day — well not quite — while the parrots dithered. We felt very dashed when they gave our lovely log cabin the thumbs down. They did not regard it as a desirable residence. A ringtail possum temporarily made it his home.

Whether or not the rosellas nest in the garden, it is still a great joy to see them flashing through the trees, or dunking themselves in the pond where the business of bathing is taken seriously. Each wing is extended as far as possible then flopped about to ensure the water gets under all the feathers. After several minutes of this body care, they fly up into an overhanging tree and spend much time in careful preening of their feathers.

Spring is a time to which we all look forward with pleasure. How often this capricious season surprises us with days of dazzling sunshine followed by howling gales and rain, which shatter tender growth and knock limbs from trees. This usually

Early Nancies in the grass.

The emblem of spring.

involves a lot of clearing up in our garden. An incredible amount of kindling results from the mayhem wrought by high winds, but we get smug satisfaction from observing the wood pile grow.

Some of the flowers in the garden that are at their best in spring are the callistemons, grevilleas, hakeas, thryptomenes and westringias. The prostantheras are covered with a generous display of flowers, as are the various forms of leptospermum, two of which are indigenous to this area, *Leptospermum continentale* and *L. lanigerum. L. laevigatum* has, of course, become identified with our coastal areas and provides an excellent windbreak and cover for little birds. Frequently, one finds small terrestrial orchids growing in the tea-tree mulch beneath them.

Anguillaria dioica (early Nancies), their fresh cream faces circled with maroon markings, dot the native grass. These belong to the lily family and are the orchid's nearest relation. Chocolate lilies, so called for their chocolate perfume, send up long sprays of purple flowers amongst the milkmaids and sundews. The latter, with their sticky dewdrop leaves and fragile little white flowers held aloft, entice unsuspecting insects to their death. Goodenias, with their yellow, upturned faces, clump in damper sections of the grass. Another little enchantress is the mauve twining fringe lily, which scrambles through the fallen bark and leaves, clinging tenaciously to everything it touches. The large fringe lily has gone from the bush around here, its haunts have been smothered by the detritus thrown up from new buildings and the introduction of invasive weeds. *Astroloma humifusum*, the cranberry heath which as children we called emu berries, bulbine lilies, dianella, hibbertia and other small plants pop up each year amongst the grass, adding great interest to the generally natural appearance of the garden.

For however long one lists the mass of spring flowers, it is impossible for me to settle on absolute favourites. The joy of spring in a bush garden is the knowledge that the flowering of native plants doesn't end at this season and the evergreen trees carry a variety of foliage which gives it continuing interest.

Summer   18

Native grasses.

A S WE GET OLDER, SUMMER IS A TIME FOR NOSTALGIA. SHARP
pangs assail us, as we remember youthful holidays spent
basking on golden beaches in endless sunshine. With our
selective memories we have obliterated all trace of cold miserable
weather, partly because the weather when you are young rarely
stops you from doing anything you set your heart on.

Nowadays, having reached the age which young people regard
as over the hill, there seems to be less and less summer weather.
Fantasies about grandchildren frisking on the beach at Christmas
are rudely dispelled! In actual fact we spent five consecutive days
with a log fire burning all day. Nevertheless, the trees and plants
soldier on, flowering at approximately the same time as usual.

Many of the melaleucas lend colour and charm to the summer
months. In our garden, *Melaleuca armillaris*, a graceful erect
shrub, puts forth white flowers in cylindrical clusters and *M.*

styphelioides, also with creamy white flowers, has prickly leaves. *M. linariifolia* is a tree with two attributes. As it ages the bark on the trunk, as with most paperbarks but more so, becomes white and furrowed and peels off to reveal all manner of intriguing holes and cracks, ideal places for bugs to inhabit and birds to probe for food. The fluffy effusion of creamy white flowers gives it its common name of snow in summer.

M. hypericifolia is a small tree or spreading bush with woody limbs. Flowers that are borne on slender arching branches are cylindrical spikes varying in colour from dull to bright red. It grows well in coastal wet places and seems hardy. But perhaps my favourite summer-flowering melaleuca is *M. nesophila*, a quick-growing dome-shaped shrub of medium texture with brittle branches. It is a very hardy shrub and withstands salt spray and strong winds. Now it is covered with flowers, mauve balls tipped with yellow, which are long lasting, eventually changing in colour to white. As with most of the wide range of melaleucas, the shrubs are attractive to the birds and respond well to pruning. A yearly autumn or winter trim is recommended.

One sometimes fails to notice the blossom up in the tops of the eucalypts. *Eucalyptus ficifolia*, that dramatic Western Australian tree, blazes with colour in late summer, in shades varying from cream through pale pink to salmon pink to bright scarlet. It attracts flocks of rainbow lorikeets, which look unbelievably brilliant as they sit sipping at the blossoms and mischievously nipping off the flower heads.

One acacia which tends to flower on and off throughout the year and is a great pleasure in summer is *Acacia retinodes* (wirilda wattle). This quick-growing tree is slender in form and has clusters of round sweet-smelling flowers. Not only is it a generous flowerer, but in our garden it seeds so that we have a constant supply of young trees coming on.

Endless lists of summer flowering trees and plants tend to be boring to the reader, so I recommend the perusal of any good books on Australian natives. These will tell you all you need to know about what is flowering in the summer months.

If we get a hot dry summer, there is the constant problem of watering. Ideally, the plants should be able to withstand the heat, but most of us attempt to grow plants not indigenous to the area and we cannot expect ferns and young newly purchased plants

Summer in the forest.

from different climates to survive. It does not always follow that even indigenous plants purchased at nurseries will thrive. For some unknown reason they sometimes die or take a long time to establish themselves. However, in the long run, the bush garden you are striving to establish will become a natural extension of the bush around you.

Watering of ferns should be done in the early morning or in the evening when the sun will not scorch the fronds. Watering of other native plants should not be undertaken in the heat of the day either; preferably, they should just be given an occasional soaking round the root system and then be heavily mulched. There is absolutely no need to drench bush gardens with continuous watering.

Some Australians, failing to recognise that we are a water-starved country, tend to grow lawns of exotic grass which require constant mowing and watering. But we have encouraged native grass to grow throughout our bush garden and the so-called lawn around the house is soft and green, gets little mowing and no watering. As the summer heat strikes, it dries off, but as soon as the rains return the whole area becomes green and grassy once more.

When the weather warms up, we sling two hammocks at a companionable distance from each other under the she-oaks, where in theory we go to read. In fact, reading is well-nigh impossible, as the constant parade of birds is totally distracting. The gentle swinging of the hammock seems not to alarm them and is soothing to the swinger within. If mosquitoes are a problem, go forth armed with suitable repellents. Every summer garden should be provided with one of those rubber-backed rugs. They are Australian made and are very useful to lie on, either at home in the garden or on picnics.

Unlike Keats, who regarded autumn as the season of mellow fruitfulness, in my mind summer evokes the thought of ripe plums, peaches and apricots. In our bush garden space has been spared for a prolific peach tree and a nectarine. Despite the nightly raids from our resident possums, we still garner a supply of delicious white fleshed peaches, the very thought of which makes my mouth water. I no longer attempt self-sufficiency in fruit and vegetables, but summer showers us with produce from our generous friends.

It is a season that I look forward to every year. There is no need to dread excessive heat, as the bush garden with its tall evergreen trees gives protection from the hot sun, and the house with its slate floors and overhanging eaves provides a cool retreat.

19 *Autumnal Thoughts*

Fungi in the woodland.

THE WORD AUTUMN HAS A SLIGHTLY MELANCHOLY RING TO it with its associations of the sere and yellow and the slow decline of fruitful years. In the autumnal bush garden, however, there is no evidence of life running down. Unlike exotic gardens, where autumn is marked by gilded leaves turning brown then dying off and trees becoming gaunt nude sculptures, in a bush garden a modicum of leaves, bark and twigs drop to the ground all the time and the trees and shrubs retain their leafy raiment all the year round. That is, of course, until old age or disease takes hold and, as no living things are immortal, inevitable death ensues.

In the part of Australia where I live, close to the sea but well sheltered from salt-laden winds, autumn is almost invariably a season of gentle warm sun, blue skies and crisp evenings, not really cold but holding the promise of wintry nights spent by a crackling fire. Perhaps of all the seasons, autumn is the most inviting for working in a garden. There are many tasks to be undertaken which prevent you from sitting inside and reading a book, unless you can quell an uneasy conscience.

In our garden in autumn, two distinctively Australian trees are flowering and provide a feast of pollen and nectar for the birds. The banksia trees, whose limbs assume cranky shapes as they lean out from coastal cliffs, balance on rocky slopes or stand revelling in swampland, are unique. May Gibbs's story of the bold, bad, banksia man has enchanted generations of Australian children. He is there for us all to see in his hairy whiskery form, peering out from the recesses of *Banksia serrata*, which is a small to medium-sized tree, with saw-toothed leaves and silvery green flowers. There are so many to choose from that, before buying banksias for your garden, it is advisable to ascertain their requirements. In our ignorance, and enthusiasm for the rare and colourful, we planted *B. menziesii*, a Western Australian beauty with red flowers. As with our hopes, it lingered on for a year or so, then gave up all pretence of struggle and died. It seems that I never learn and continue to try and make plants conform to an environment not their own. Perhaps old age will temper my foolish expectations.

Two indigenous banksias, *B. integrifolia* and *B. marginata*, grow in our bush garden but, irritatingly, the latter never looks half as handsome as the specimens on the shore. There they are battered by sea winds, have barely a toehold it would seem in the sand, look glossy and are covered with glorious 15 centimetre long flower cones of gleaming gold.

B. ericifolia and *B. spinulosa* have both thrived in our garden. The new flowers of *B. spinulosa* have golden tresses which are imprisoned by black hairpins, restraining them into long crimped cylindrical heads filled with nectar. The honey-eaters feast on this nectar which is replenished daily. Slender leaves with tiny serrated edges grow out in a spray, whilst embedded in the old wood are last season's seed pods. These resemble fat brown fibre-covered cones, in which chocolate lozenges are embedded. *B. ericifolia* has delicate heath-like leaves and sports beautiful glowing orange or rufous cones excellent for flower arrangement.

As I write, it is the last month of autumn and a grey thrush has alighted briefly on a branch outside the window. He hops along the branches, searching for food. His colouring is perfectly adapted for camouflage. The top of his body is a combination of soft litter-browns and grey, very like the she-oaks he frequents and, until he moves, he is not very noticeable. His underside is pearl grey like many of the eucalypt tree trunks in the garden and he has a large round enquiring eye.

Later in the morning I hear a young thrush practising its song. After a few moments, the parent flies into a neighbouring tree to correct the phrasing. Music goes backwards and forwards between the two trees, the young bird improvises and the parent attempts to restrain its virtuoso flights of fancy by sticking to one melodic line. Maybe I am anthropomorphising yet again, but it is for us humans such a delight to listen to the music making of the birds, who do not have to go through the arduous process of learning how to produce their voices. Not for them the business of diaphragmatic breathing, controlling their emotions, articulating clearly and learning foreign tongues; they just open their beaks and let the sound pour forth.

Autumn is the flowering season for the casuarinas in our garden and to my mind they are one of the loveliest trees to grow. There are species ranging from trees of 18 metres to low-growing shrubs. Found in such disparate places as desert, swampland, mountain and coastal regions, they all share the simple grace of delicate green branchlets which, on the male tree, become tassels dusted with orange and gold pollen in the autumn. Both male and female trees bear flowers. The female flowers are made up of small tufts of red pistils with a glistening dewy look, which is quite charming. These small flowers later develop into wonderful seed cones, like a tubby echidna minus legs and questing nose. They look dramatic ranging along the branches against the skyline. A small grove of casuarinas can transform a garden and the falling needles make the most perfect mulch for any native plant. Children are intrigued to find that the needles can be pulled apart at the tiny joints and then fitted together again, no glue needed! *Casuarina torulosa* (rose she-oak) has a special charm for me. To begin with, the trunk and branches of this medium to large tree have corky bark and are greatly enjoyed by all manner of birds and bugs who forage there. It has a graceful weeping habit and the foliage, as suggested by its name, is tinged a soft rosy red, especially on the young growth.

Banksia integrifolia.

Eucalyptus forrestiana.

Another of the joys of late autumn in a bush garden arrives with the onset of rain. After many weeks of near drought, the blessed rain descends and within a day mushrooms are pushing up small mounds of dirt to reveal their creamy speckled domes. All sizes and many forms abound from trumpet-shaped cones to fairy sized tables and stools with permanently pleated underskirts of pale creams and browns. Sandy soil, smothered with leaf mould from the she-oaks, seems to be a favoured place for them.

A rather testing moment in my life was experienced when some European friends, with a knowledge of fungi far greater than mine, pounced with glad cries upon the little bright orange toadstools that popped up their gay parasols around the garden. Fried in butter and presented to me on small squares of bread, good manners required that I try them. With heart and fungus in mouth, I swallowed my first toadstool and lived to tell the tale. I do not suggest that people collect fungi to eat unless they are experts in the field, better to stick to the tried and tested mushroom that you know. There is something infinitely satisfying about picking delicacies from your own garden, such as home-grown mushrooms that are a free gift from nature.

Because of an exceptionally dry April and consistently warmer weather than ever before recorded in the State of Victoria, I am reluctantly watering some plants on a regular basis. In theory, my bush garden should be fending for itself, taking the rough with the smooth, the wet with the dry, and demonstrating the survival of the fittest. Well, that would be fine if the gardener was made of sterner stuff and did not get carried away with ill-advised planting.

Prostanthera ovalifolia, although not indigenous to this area, is one of my favourite mint bushes and not only grows well in our garden, but pays us the infinite compliment of regularly sending up quite a number of seedlings. If I do not restrain my transplantings, the garden will be a gush of purple in the spring. However, there are unexpected checks and balances in a bush garden and in the drought, our mint bushes are the first to suffer. Very quickly they close up their leaves and droop despondently and, if I don't water them thoroughly, death will ensue. That is not really a reflection on the plant, but on our poor soil which will not retain moisture and was not designed for *P. ovalifolia*. Apart from the ferns in the garden and various pots round the house, we try not to water any other plants.

Someone who is relishing the extended period of warmth is a small brown skink, that beautifully formed little reptile who will adventure into the house through some small opening. One found its way into the dangerous and slippery confines of a handbasin. As I was afraid of damaging its small body, it had to wait there until a less faint-hearted friend came and returned it to the big wide world outside. Another turned up spread-eagled against a cream curtain, which made me think what a charming design it would make on indoor fabrics. He was allowed to find his own way out when he was ready. These visitors make one feel happily part of our immensely varied bushlife.

The small shrublet, *Crowea exalata*, is a dependable attractive plant which flowers from summer through autumn to winter. It grows in sandy soils or cool forests and its pink 1 to 2 centimetre starry flowers are long-lasting in a vase. *Grevillea* 'Robyn Gordon' is a mainstay in any garden, where it will flower not only in autumn, but every other season of the year. Its generous trusses of red flowers keep coming and it responds well to pruning, thus avoiding a straggly appearance. Mine does not approve of being picked for floral arrangements and instantly droops its head when placed in a vase.

The little *Viola hederacea* flowers valiantly in our garden, competing bravely with grass, *Dichondra repens* and weeds such as the dreaded small oxalis. Fortunately, the latter tends to die down over the summer months, allowing the little native violets to get a good grip. Surely one of the most tedious tasks in the garden is that of trying to weed out oxalis. Each horrid little bulb has to be pulled out carefully and put in a bucket to be destroyed. For every one you pull out, ten seem to appear, but it must be attempted otherwise your bush garden will become a sea of innocent little white flower faces in the spring.

While *Acacia iteaphylla* and *A. retinodes* are the only two wattles in flower in our garden during autumn, there are a whole array of different wattles whose buds are bursting with the promise of flowers to come. The grevilleas, too, are covered in buds. Some, such as the striking *Grevillea dimorpha*, are already in flower, their fiery red spider flowers gleaming amongst the olive-green leaves.

In autumn we get visits at night from two species of large moths, who batter themselves at the windows in a vain attempt to reach the source of light. One, the emperor gum moth, is large and has intricate markings in russet and brown tonings on its wings, whilst its furry feelers are dark grey. The other species is the goat moth, a soft kid-grey creature with a wavy dark grey line down the surface of its wings. Sometimes at night, as I sit by the uncurtained window, a great shape comes swooping out of the darkness to snatch the unsuspecting moth. It is the tawny frogmouth capturing an easy supper. I hope the moth suffers less than it does from its self-inflicted battering on the glass.

Winter Cheer *20*

A New Holland honeyeater
at a banksia.

THE ENGLISH POET, WORDSWORTH, CLAIMED THAT 'STERN
Winter loves a dirge-like sound', but then he didn't know
about our Australian winters. Although we get fogs, frosts
and rain in winter, we also expect to have many crisp and sunny
days. Nor do we suffer the gloom of darkness settling like a pall
over everything by mid-afternoon. We are indeed a lucky country
with regard to the climate and for another important reason.

Many of our native trees and plants come into bloom in
midwinter. The trees never lose their leaves and we can be
excused for thinking that the garden we are surveying in winter is
a spring garden. Most of our birds are not forced to seek warmer
climes to survive, but continue to find plenty of food in the
native bush. While one understands the need to feed the shivering
robins in an English snowscape, our birds are perfectly capable of
fending for themselves. Unlike household pets, a licence is not

required for us to keep them and we can leave them at any time without a care, knowing that on our return they will be here to welcome us. They are the greatest bonus a garden can give, and an overgrown bush garden gives them nothing but joy.

Another winter pleasure comes from lighting a fire in the hearth. We all love the smell of the woodsmoke as it weaves its way up the chimney and disperses into the bleak, cold outdoor air. In some respects, winter storms make one quail as the trees lash and creak and sometimes a branch cracks and falls, but the damage is usually repairable and the bonus of extra firewood eases the pain. In our bush garden the supply of wood has been continuous over thirty years and only once have we bought a load of firewood. To be truthful, we have also had the doubtful pleasure of collecting wood from the wholesale amputation of trees on the roadside, apparently seen as a necessary precaution by higher authorities but regarded as verging on ruthless enthusiasm by those of us who watch the trees being cut down and disfigured. 'It's an ill wind' that replenishes our firewood but wracks our sensibilities.

There has been a sharp sudden downpour of rain and now the sun is shining. This is a picture no artist can paint. Every leaf on every tree and shrub is spangled with glinting diamonds and the birds have burst into song. As quickly as it has happened, the sun disappears again and the garden assumes its modest variations of green raiment. It is never dull.

A flock of silver gulls freewheel over the garden uttering their harsh, drawn-out cries, but never landing in the garden. This immaculate white bird, with grey back and brilliant scarlet bill and legs, is common to the whole of the Australian coastline. Their calls are evocative of all those sunlit memories we have of sandy beaches, with toddlers advancing boldly on a gathering of gulls, pieces of bread squashed tight in fat little hands.

Mosses start to thicken in the grass even before the winter rains begin. Dew seems to provide sufficient dampness to produce green velvet cushions on rocks and logs. The slowly disintegrating wooden steps on the paths are rimmed with moss and fat orange honey fungi, like piled up plates of golden pikelets, make their appearance at the foot of several dying she-oaks. There are over 100,000 different kinds of fungi in the world, ranging from microscopic moulds and mildews to large toadstools, mushrooms

Leptospermum macrocarpum.

A variety of wattles.

and puffballs, which is a mind-boggling statistic. In our bush garden there is a modest selection, including a strange black club-like growth and a puffball which starts life looking like a fleshy flower with reflexed curving petals. A rainbow coloured fungus appears on dead wood and various other forms of fungi surprise me each winter.

In one small fern section of the garden, under an overhanging *Acacia floribunda* and a red-flowering *Grevillea victoriae*, I have secreted a bromeliad planted in a pot, the latter heavily disguised with rock and rotting wood. To my joy it has sent up long sprays of magenta flowers which later turn bright blue and will last well into the winter. I have seen this particular bromeliad growing naturally in northern Queensland and feel very impressed that it has flowered in our garden, albeit in a pot and not on the trunk of a tree. I don't dare to transfer it for fear of losing it.

Two hakeas are in flower in the first month of winter, *Hakea laurina* and *H. sericea*. As mentioned before, the pincushion flowers of the former and the pink mist of the latter provide a source of nectar and security to the birds.

Acacia iteaphylla is in flower, as is the glorious *A. baileyana*, which provides a sheet of gold in my neighbour's garden and for me a stunning sight from my bedroom window. *A. acinacea*, a charming small tree which grows up to 2 metres, is covered in small pale golden blossom and is another winter flowerer. It rejoices in the name of gold-dust wattle and thrives in an open situation. Late winter finds *A. boormanii*, *A. pravissima*, *A. podalyrifolia* and *A. retinodes* in flower in the garden. These are just a few of the favourites which should warm any heart in winter.

Banksia ericifolia, *B. integrifolia*, *B. marginata* and *B. spinulosa* are flowering, as is *Bauera rubioides*, that charmer of creek banks and moist gullies, which is covered in dainty mauve flowers. Correas are launching into their long-flowering season at the beginning of winter. The vivid red reflexed tubular bells, sometimes tipped in yellow or green, of *Correa reflexa* are eye-catching. It has a green form, too, called forest correa, which is indigenous to the area where we live. *C. pulchella* is a variable small shrub to 1 metre high, with shiny, heart-shaped leaves and pendant orange-red bells in winter and spring.

The delightfully scented shrub *Cassia nemophila* also flowers in my garden in winter. Its bright yellow flowers hang like bells from the stalk-like leaflets and its foliage makes a distinct contrast to other plants. It likes a dry well drained and sunny situation.

One of the most stunning of the small eucalypts, *Eucalyptus caesia*, opens its red-pink flowers in midwinter. Even when not in flower, this is a delicious tree which has a waxy white and powdery bloom covering its upper stems and buds. A copse of these small trees provide year-long enchantment.

21 *Simple Pleasures*

The gentle native violet.

DESPITE THE OBVIOUS NEED FOR SOME SERIOUS AND MAJOR works to be undertaken in our bush garden, on a cool and blustery day I decided to indulge myself in simple pleasures. The maidenhair, which has naturalised in many parts of the garden, originated from two or three very small clumps. Having quite frequently admired wonderful displays of maidenhair growing in pots in my friends' homes, I decided it was time my bathroom was similarly adorned. Digging up two small clumps and disentangling them from the roots of the melaleuca under which they were growing, I planted them in plastic pots, placing one in an old glazed Swedish vase, the other in a black clay pot ornamented with Egyptian-looking decorations. Although the plants are quite small at the moment, in my mind's eye I see them billowing over the sides of their containers. The need to feed or not to feed them is something yet to be decided upon.

The next gentle task was to convert a hanging fern basket into a swinging bird pool. Kind friends have at times given me hanging baskets, but I seem to have a dead hand where they are concerned. Nothing retains its air of healthy rapture and, and no matter what I do, few plants survive. Perhaps the plants sense that my heart isn't in their future. Whatever it is, I have decided to use a little lateral thinking. To what other use could I put this large hanging basket? A friend suggested planting small native violets round the edge and sinking a bird bath in the centre of the basket. Having completed this simple operation (as native violets run riot in my garden, there was no dearth of small plants), I placed a few stones and some water in the terracotta dish and hung the whole creation from a low branch of the *Casuarina torulosa*, with plenty of close protective tree cover for the birds. Now I shall sit by the window and watch for the first brave spirit to investigate the new watering hole.

As I was looking round for a terracotta dish to place in the hanging basket, I found two small seedlings of *Eucalyptus viminalis* growing up in the mulch round an existing bird pool stand. As the verge of our bush garden still has room for a couple of indigenous trees, these little seedlings were carefully transplanted. I mulched them well with tea-tree litter and marked each one with a stake, watered it well and breathed a prayer for its long and lusty life.

By now I was feeling a warm inner glow but no physical heat. So, when another simple pleasure presented itself, I was off again, this time to the large woodheap which sports a tidy cut log section and an enormous heap of sawn-off boughs and branches. Hunting in this pile, I was looking for a long forked branch to prop up the archway over the path down the bank. For some years the trunks and branches of the *Melaleuca ericifolia* have been supporting an ever-increasingly exuberant *Pandorea jasminoides*, whose glossy green leaves very quickly covered the framework of melaleuca. The white trumpet-like flowers have a deep crimson throat and hang in clusters, flowering profusely and making a glorious sight from spring, through summer to autumn. If I was not to have the arch collapsing under the weight of this lovely creeper, urgent support was needed. A long piece of sturdy wattle with several convenient forks was put in place and for the moment, all is well.

As I worked quietly at my simple tasks, the bush cleaners were at work. Little silvereyes and thornbills, less strident and just as efficient as vacuum cleaners, were travelling up and down the leaves of many trees and plants in the garden, devouring scale and small insects that can be harmful to the foliage. There is no need for sprays in a bush garden, where the birds do all the cleaning up that is necessary for healthy growth. The silvereyes have a pleasant warbling song and a high-pitched 'chew', and the thornbills sing sweetly, their song changing to a churring sound if alarmed.

Occasionally I spot the revolting black clusters of sawfly larvae in a gum tree. Gang-gangs are said to eat them but, before the grubs can demolish the leaves, I confess to knocking them off the tree into a bucket and murdering them. I suppose they have their place in the balance of nature, but for me the life of my young gum trees is of paramount importance. I feel rather sick after the slaughter, I have to admit, and wonder what useful purpose these strange creatures serve. They smell very strongly of eucalyptus when crushed.

My day of simple pleasures was crowned by the discovery that *Eucalyptus ficifolia* had burst into flower. Not one but five of these lovely trees from Western Australia, we have planted in the last thirty years, full of high hopes for sheets of glowing colour. The first one pined, could I say, in the shade of a neighbour's pine tree and for many years refused to grow. When eventually the pine tree was removed it shot up, healthy and glad to be alive. After two or three years it still had not flowered, but looked very strong. Then came disaster. Suddenly it sickened for no apparent reason, turned up its toes and died. Three others did quite well, but all produced white flowers. I wanted deep rose-red or salmon-pink flowers, not white. Now I have what I hoped for.

Last year this particular *E. ficifolia* flowered for the first time and the blossoms were not much more than white. They had the merest tinge of pink. But on this lovely day it is covered with icing pink blossoms and my joy is unconfined. The bees love it and so do I.

Eucalyptus ficifolia.

Casuarina torulosa.

22 *Mysteries of the Compost Heap*

The workshop.

BECAUSE OF A THRIFTY STREAK IN MY NATURE DUE MAYBE to some Scottish ancestry, I do enjoy getting something for nothing; hence I spent a happy hour this winter's day collecting mulch. The roof of the workshop and the chook house had become nearly ankle deep in rotting she-oak needles, before I whipped myself into action. Sweeping the roofs clean, I carted barrow loads of this black rotting mass to the compost. Even at this stage, several pink worms were visible amongst the needles which had been heaping up on the tin roof. How did they get there?

Many of us are compost experts, producing rich dark tilth, that feels and smells good and is alive with worms. There is another type of composter, to whose company I belong, who is rather more slapdash than scientific, but whose whole gardening experience is enriched by the exciting unpredictability of the compost heap. Not for us the measured application of lime or blood and bone, or layers of this and that, just a glorious profusion of every form of vegetable matter, manure or liquid, that comes to hand.

After the heap has grown to a certain height, I start undermining the structure to get at the rotted soil. The sighting of moist pink worms is greeted with joy, as they are the best of all composters. Used mainly for building up existing banks, incorporating into the soil for new plantings, or giving extra nourishment to special plants, the ritual spreading of this magic soil is very satisfying, but it is as nothing compared to the excitement, in a couple of weeks' time, of discovering all manner of seedlings making their appearance. A veritable kitchen garden can be achieved in this way—pumpkins, tomatoes, zucchini, butternut pumpkins, green and red peppers, silverbeet, nectarines and peaches. A cornucopia and all for free!

The sight of a large orange and yellow pumpkin displayed prominently on the sideboard at dinner is a good conversation booster when it is modestly claimed that its humble origin was the compost heap. You soon flush out the gardeners from the rest.

Maybe a more scientific approach might produce a greater proportion of soil as opposed to a variety of strange half-rotted lumps and undigested roots, but for my money it's all good mulch, with the added bonus of delightful and diverse seedlings for the garden.

As we still had hankerings after subsistence living, largely repressed, we once decided to grow our own eggs and enjoy the sight of chickens in the garden. We built a low-roofed shed onto the back of the workshop and erected a high wire fence enclosing a good sized jungle of grass. Buying the chooks was rather like my impulse buying of plants. We were very charmed at the market by various varieties of birds with handsome feathers and guaranteed about to lay. Well, they did look charming and occasionally dropped an egg or two into the nests, but were really not much more than an ornament to the garden. After their demise some years later, we took a more hard-headed approach to chooks and bought white Orpingtons. These poor creatures had started life in a battery and their beaks had been cut off. It was pathetic to watch their first days of freedom. They had no idea how to jump up onto the perches, nor could they manage to eat the seed heads on the grass and thistles. Over the next few days, it was a delight to watch as they mastered the arts of hopping, scratching in the ground and, best of all, taking dust baths. They were like deprived children being given the keys to paradise.

Apart from the eggs which they began to deliver with great regularity, we had another bounty—chook manure which, with ground-up eggshells, became a luxurious additive to the compost heap. There is a sad postscript to this story. Some years later a fox managed to climb up the fence and, in a night of horrendous slaughter and mayhem, bit the head off every chook. There they lay, dead in a sea of white feathers. That was the end of our fowl enterprise, no pun intended.

During the summer months we tend to accumulate a lot of newspapers and, as there are no fires to be tended, newspaper goes on to the compost too. I tear it up a bit so that it gets spread through the rest of the compost and in no time it rots down, all adding to that environmentally friendly fertiliser that we can manufacture ourselves. A warning for those who throw their weeds onto the compost; never allow the bulbs of oxalis or onion grass, or pieces of wandering jew, to get in with the rest of the refuse, or you will live to regret it. They are the most damnable of all enemies to a gardener and seem indestructible.

If I discover a worm under a garden pot, I hurry earnestly to the compost heap with it wriggling madly in my fist. There I inter it most gently, hoping for a thousandfold increase of its number. The gentle art of composting gives one a feeling of working with nature, wasting nothing that is of value and providing cost-free nourishment for the garden.

Workshop in the bush.

23 *Other Gardens and Influences*

Butterfly and bull ant.

OR THOSE OF US WITH NO BACKGROUND IN GARDENING AND
for whom the prospect of making a first garden seems
quite daunting, there are many avenues to explore which
will quickly dispel all feelings of inadequacy. Many books which
can be found in local libraries or bookshops, have been written
on all forms of gardens, trees, shrubs and flowers.

Two slim paperback books written by Betty Maloney and Jean
Walker galvanised us into action. *Designing Bush Gardens* and
More About Bush Gardens were not only written most beautifully, but were packed with simple and compelling directions for
making a bush garden. They became our Bible and we pored over
them, then rushed outside to put the ideas into practice. Sadly,
these books are now out of print, but I recommend them to
anyone who can lay their hands on a copy.

If book buying is too expensive, a quick and careful browse

through some of the garden books on display is seldom frowned upon by booksellers, for there is always the prospect that you will become so hooked on gardening that book buying will supplant some other form of expenditure.

Having read as many books as you can get your hands on, visiting plant nurseries is a most inspiring, tantalising and stimulating way to spend your weekends. Taking a pad and pencil with you is the best way to commit to memory the names and descriptions of form, colour and habit of all the plants which particularly take your fancy. You need to take a little time over deciding on their suitability or otherwise, if your garden is still at the planning stage. Some people, such as the writer of this treatise, don't always practise what they preach and after thirty years are still trying to fool themselves. 'Just one more try at growing a waratah,' I say to myself, and then suffer pangs of disappointment as it slowly expires.

Some native plant nurseries are beautifully landscaped to give the illusion of being within the framework of the bush. In them you can see plants growing in a natural setting, which is very helpful in providing inspiration for your own efforts at bush gardening. One native nursery that I visit has another attraction. There is, at all times of the year, an immense arrangement of many-coloured flowers placed in a rustic office. It is an example of the diversity we can get from our Australian flower species which bloom prolifically throughout the year.

In recent years there has been a growing interest in trying to restore some of the beauty that once belonged to our urban river frontages. Replanting with indigenous trees and shrubs along the banks and round the billabongs, is doing a great deal to enhance degraded areas. 'Man makes a death which nature never made.' So wrote the poet Edward Young back in the eighteenth century. I wonder what he would have thought of twentieth century man. I suspect he would have been rendered speechless.

One gardener, whose progress I have watched with admiration, became vitally concerned with regenerating the bush on his suburban block by the river Yarra. His garden starts on a level plane around the house. At the back, it slopes down gradually then more precipitously to the river. This is where he has taken up the challenge of regenerating the bush.

Indigenous plants are part of our biological heritage and are a unique and irreplaceable attribute. Their preservation retains locally rare gene pools and provides wildlife habitat for insects, reptiles, birds and butterflies. Imported soil, water (apart from some initial watering), fertiliser, insecticides and herbicides are not needed; therefore the use of indigenous species in the garden has resource, conservation and economic benefits.

The only indigenous plants on this river site were a few small lightwoods, black wattle, sweet bursaria, kangaroo apple and two callistemons. The whole area was covered with a collection of sixty-two species of 'weeds', ranging from pepper trees, pine trees and pampas grass to agapanthus, angled onion, soursob and petty spurge — wonderful names but fearsome adversaries.

Some may take issue with the description of well-loved plants as weeds, but by definition in the Oxford dictionary, a weed is 'a herbaceous plant, not valued for use or beauty and growing wild or rank, especially as hindering growth of more valued plants'. I rest my case.

Before anything else could be done, the large trees had to be cut down and the weeds carefully removed without resort to spraying. Tackling a section at a time, the owner cleared a space then mulched thickly. Fitting in wooden sleepers and dry rock walls to retain the soil and angling bluestone steps winding down towards the river across the slope, he planted heavily with indigenous trees for the over-storey, shrubs, then native grasses, rushes, reeds, lilies and other small plants. The ultimate aim was to create a relatively open woodland effect.

The elegance of a clump of kangaroo grass with its bronze seed heads waving in the breeze is something to marvel at, as is the sculptural sturdiness of reeds and lilies appearing to grow out of rock.

Some years later, great changes could be seen. Where once there was a mat of wandering jew, ivy, blue periwinkle and Cape weed, there are now fifteen species of tall waving native grasses. Some bear feathery plumes, some hold spears aloft and others spring from silky tussocks. There are flax lilies and chocolate lilies, ferns and groundsel. Seaberry saltbush sprawls over the rock faces and bluebells start out of crevices in the rock steps. The red-faced, out of breath, running postman and the common flat pea share a warm spot with the scrambling purple coral pea.

River red gums, yellow box and seven other members of the

Flannel flowers in Judy Watts' garden.

The brilliance of callistemons.

Myrtacea family are growing apace, whist *Clematis microphylla* (small-leafed clematis) is twining affectionately through everything it can embrace.

Hundreds of plantings have been made. There have been some deaths, but the excitement of witnessing the regeneration of many plants and the seeding of others is great. It is a big job, but a grand example of what can be done to help restore to its original beauty the degraded banks of a river.

It would be wonderful if those who are fortunate enough to own river frontages could combine in an effort of restoration that would produce a corridor of indigenous bushland to delight all living creatures and to be a gift to posterity.

Another splendid bush garden, where I stayed overnight, surrounds a mud-brick house in a north Victorian country town. Situated on a half acre block, this garden enfolds you as quietly and naturally as does the 'real' bush. The house has a slate-floored garden room somewhat like a conservatory adjoining the living room, out of which grows a beautiful gum tree. There being no roof, the many plants grow in unfettered beauty, in pots and between the slates. The garden is largely planted with eucalypts and she-oaks, including one spectacular *Casuarina torulosa* (rough barked forest oak). When I was there, this tall specimen was covered from top to toe in a rosy-rust coloured shawl of incredible splendour. *Eucalyptus citriodora* (lemon-scented gum) has taken the environment to its heart and continually sends up young saplings which contribute to a small forest. *Casuarina cristata*, an erect tree with pale grey-green branchlets, sends up suckers and forms little copses.

Underneath the trees, which come right up to the house, there is a deep litter of leaves, twigs and some rotting logs. There is not a great deal of underplanting, but dianella, eremophila and other small herbaceous plants push their way through. This garden was made by someone who used both artistry and restraint to achieve a deeply restful and natural surrounding for her home. Many birds such as gang gangs, little friar birds, black-faced cuckoo shrikes and ravens are attracted to the tall trees and some make their nests there.

Forty years ago I saw my first bush garden in the heart of Melbourne. A white weatherboard house, sitting on a small block of land in a rather conservative suburb, drew me like a magnet as I wheeled my baby out for his daily airing. The front garden was composed of tall gums and a few wattles; the ground beneath covered in leaves, bark and seed pods. Although I have forgotten the details of this small garden, the impression it made on me has never faded. It was planted by Miss Helen Waddell, a botanist who was deeply involved in the natural habitat and who was far ahead of her time. Such natural beauty made the surrounding gardens look rather sad and dreary by comparison.

It is always inspiring to see bush gardens which are strikingly successful. There is such a one in Langwarrin. Here the soil is deep sand and the perfect medium, not only for the many indigenous plants and trees, but in this garden for spectacular sheets of flannel flowers. Each year they seed thickly and, together with the white flowered wedding bush, which blooms at the same time, it makes an unforgettable sight.

In their ten acre bush garden, they have built a wonderful lake, complete with an island which looks totally natural and, of course, draws water birds, frogs and many other water-loving creatures to its shores.

All these bush gardeners have worked with nature to produce a priceless habitat which, one hopes, will inspire and influence other gardeners to do the same.

24 *Introducing Children to Bush Gardening*

Trigger plant.

INTRODUCING CHILDREN TO THE EXCITEMENT AND BEAUTY of the bush seems to me to be something we need to do at a very early age. They are naturally curious creatures and love to make collections of every sort of thing so it is easy to interest a little child in the shape and feel of objects such as sea-shells, stones, leaves, nuts and seed pods. If we leave this introduction to an age where they are at school, there are many competing interests to distract them and peer pressure is strong. To prefer a walk in the bush to a game of sport can mark a child out as different, perhaps odd. This is gradually changing, I am glad to say, and schools are doing a lot to interest children in the care of their environment, which is an urgent necessity if the beauty and diversity of our planet is to survive.

Looking for animals and birds on a bush walk can take on the attributes of a treasure hunt. The first person to sight a koala reclining in the fork of a tree feels a flush of pride! Learning to walk quietly and watch for movement in the trees will often provide the thrill of discovering an unusual bird.

Some adult bushwalkers tend to stride at a great rate along bush tracks, their eyes, apart from an occasional glance at a wristwatch, set straight ahead. Rather than taking time out to linger over a plant or focus on the bird life in the trees, the aim, it seems, is to cover as much ground as possible in the shortest time. This surely defeats the whole purpose of walking in the bush.

There are many plants to intrigue children, and the unusual mechanisms that some plants employ to gain nourishment are fascinating. In our bush garden we have two species of the little perennial sundew. These herbs are carnivorous, and the thought of such innocent looking little plants trapping insects and absorbing their juices for nourishment appeals to the bloodthirsty young. The insects land on the dewy leaves of the plant and are trapped. The hairs of the plant bend inwards, squashing the insect against the leaf. As sundews usually grow in nitrogen-deficient soil, the plants gain supplementary food and energy from the insects. One variety in our garden, *Drosera whittakeri*, has a pure white five-petalled flower which sits on top of a radical rosette of green or reddish glistening leaves. When fully open, the flowers almost cover the rosette of leaves and are very fragrant. The other species, which appears in profusion in late winter and early spring, is *D. binata*, which has smaller, more delicate flowers, held aloft in a branched cluster at the end of an erect flower stalk. Like the majority of sundews, both grow in damp, sandy soils.

Another wildflower which is a hit with children is *Stylidium graminifolium* (grass trigger plant). There are 136 species of stylidium worldwide and we have four species on the Mornington peninsula. *S. graminifolium* delighted me when, after some years spent preserving our native grass and wildflower patch, it suddenly appeared amongst the leaf litter in an open space between the trees. The flower stalks are 20 to 60 centimetres long and bear terminal white, pink or magenta flowers, which are in bloom from October to February.

The way in which pollen is transferred from the anthers to the stigma, causing fertilisation of the flower, attains the status of an art form in the trigger plant. When an insect lands on the slender trigger-like bent column of the flower, the column springs up as its sensitive base is touched. Insects, which visit the flower in its early development, receive a deposit of pollen when struck by the trigger and when later on they visit a flower in which the stigma is receptive, this will also strike the insect, gathering up the pollen which was collected previously. It is all high plant technology!

Children can set off the trigger by gently touching the centre of the flower with a blade of grass. This always causes amusement and does not harm the plant, as the trigger re-sets itself in its own good time.

There are many seed pods of banksias, gum nuts, hakeas and she-oak cones which lend themselves to children's play, but the best of them all are the witches' fingers found on *Eucalyptus conferruminata*, which for many years was incorrectly sold as *E. lehmannii*. The latter is a species with much smaller buds, flowers and fruits. As the flower opens in a burst of yellow stamens, the curious, curved round fingers which have enclosed it drop off. They fit most perfectly on children's fingers and give rise to many dramatic games.

Sometimes we have difficulty trying to choose presents for our children for a birthday or for Christmas. There is a welter of state-of-the-art battery-powered toys and space-age creatures to tempt us, mostly very expensive and requiring constant re-energising.

As gardeners, imbued with the love of plants and flowers, perhaps we could look at a simple alternative. Children are by nature creative and respond to the idea of digging, delving and planting. Selecting a small plot in the garden, preferably where there is sunlight, and setting it aside entirely for the child is a good start. Together with this gift of land could come a small trowel, fork, watering can, packets of seed and a tray of seedlings. With a judicious amount of help and lots of praise, most children quickly become intrigued with the project and proud of their efforts, making decorative edges to their gardens and waiting impatiently for the first seeds to appear.

Another intriguing present is a magnifying glass. This opens up a whole world of marvels. Having exhausted all the possibilities of looking into your eyes and ears, fingernails and teeth, they can be lured out into the garden to look at the shape and colouring of insects, seed pods, flowers and leaves, all appearing quite remarkable.

Seed pods of the Flinders Ranges wattle.

She-oak cones.

Some children like to grow vegetables and have the satisfaction of bringing them to the table to be eaten. Others like to grow a mixture of herbs and colourful flowers. They can be introduced to the idea of enriching the soil with compost, which they can help to make. In the process there will be the exciting discovery of delicious, pink and wriggly worms. They will also need to learn the art of watering, neither too much nor too little, otherwise the seeds and seedlings will suffer either a soggy death or a thirsty one.

However they choose to make their gardens, it is never too early to start encouraging children to be planters. This will set their feet on a path to endless pleasure, open their eyes to the miracle of nature and solve the problem of present giving.

At nightfall, warmly wrapping a young child in a blanket and carrying it outside in your arms, is a lovely introduction to the mysteries of the universe. The scientists tell us that we are all children of the stars, created from a speck of stardust in the mists of time, and this enchanting thought becomes very real when we look up into the unfathomable night sky. To see a flock of ibis, flying in V-formation across the moon, adds yet another dimension of beauty to the scene. At the risk of sounding tedious, I feel passionate about children growing up to see the beauty in our world. We can't protect them from hideous realities but we can give them a treasure trove to store in their hearts and minds.

Building cubby houses and climbing trees are two occupations enjoyed by children. When our young son built his first cubby house, the neighbour was heard to ask him if he was moving out. On one of our many camping trips into the wilds of New South Wales, we built a very superior mia mia for our labrador dog. The entrance to it was placed close to the campfire and he lay inside, looking out with a dreamy and contented expression. When we returned a year later, the mia mia was still undisturbed and intact. Such simple pleasures make camping in the bush one of the best ways to holiday with children. It is inexpensive and very different from our day to day living in the cities. Close contact with the bush rubs off on children and more and more families are experiencing this rewarding type of holiday.

I still remember, when I was young, being absorbed in the making of a miniature garden. This is another simple pleasure for children to experience, requiring little more than a shallow container of some description filled with earth. Give the child the idea of constructing a little house made of sticks with a bark roof and poke leafy twigs into the earth to resemble trees; use a trickle of sand to make a winding pathway and a small shell filled with water for a pond; pebbles for rocks, tiny flowers and clumps of moss, all spark the imagination and can lead to artistic creations. It is another way to nurture love and awareness of the world around us.

25 *The End of the Story*

A flock of ibis.

THE JOY OF BUSH GARDENING IS RATHER LIKE A LONG-lasting love affair. While you can't expect everyone to be riveted by your experience, it is reasonable to hope that some of your happiness will be communicated to others. The charms and the character of one's garden, so obvious to oneself, may not be perceived in quite the same light by other observers, but it is a case of 'unto thine own self be true'. If we happen to believe that we have an obligation to try and preserve all the species we have inherited on this planet, then this is one way to help achieve this aim to a greater or lesser degree. Thirty-one years after the purchase of our first little block of land, hundreds of plants now thrive on it and over fifty species of birds have contributed their full measure of visual and aural delight.

Those of us who love the modest ways of many of our Australian wildflowers find it hard to witness the wholesale destruction of so much of their habitat. It seems difficult to alert people to the treasures that exist on their newly acquired land and it is sad to see how the bulldozer is given carte blanche when a new home is being constructed. With a little forethought and exploration, many small plants can be found and safely potted and whole areas roped off to prevent the ravages of building, thus preserving some of the precious species that are fast disappearing.

It is a source of constant interest each year to discover in our woodland garden the reappearance of small terrestrial orchids. Sometimes only the leaves appear and at other times, as in this year, a small patch of *Corybas dilatatus* (veined helmet orchid) flowered for the first time. When the long brown stem of the orchid *Gastrodia sesamoides* (cinnamon bells) appeared I could hardly believe my eyes. Never before, in twenty-nine years of our garden, had I seen them. I kept going back to look at the leafless treasure with its cluster of curved cinnamon bells, each with a white mouth, just to make sure that it was not a dream.

Crawling round on hands and knees, looking for spider orchids, nodding greenhoods and mosquito orchids amongst the grass, is like a treasure hunt with its attendant thrills and disappointments. *Microtis unifolia* (onion orchid) reappears faithfully every year, but brown beaks, donkey orchids, pink fairies and parson's bands have not been seen for several years. Maybe they will surprise us by coming again some day.

Some nurserymen are now propagating wildflowers and, if we all grow a few in our gardens, we will be helping to preserve some of the species which are in danger of being lost forever. There are many splendid books on Australian wildflowers, faithfully illustrated and with information about the regions from which they come. It is not difficult to re-create in one's own garden, the sort of habitat that these plants require.

Says the seventeenth century poet, Dr Walter Pope,

'May I govern my passion with an absolute sway,
And grow wiser and better as my strength wears away.'

He could have been talking about the so-called gentle art of gardening, which tends to become a passion that rules our lives, regardless of our strength. I spend a considerable amount of time upside down in my garden, endeavouring to extricate plants from a tangle of riotous weeds, grass and creepers. Whether the attendant rush of blood to the head produces more cerebral activity than usual, I am not sure, but I find myself thinking increasingly of the future. Mind you, the groaning and creaking of protesting joints has a bit to do with it, too, as I contemplate some of the things I can manage no longer.

We are so conditioned to accepting the equation that order equals beauty in the garden, that we become slaves to maintenance. No fence must sag under the weight of a rampant creeper, no edging should remain untrimmed. Weeds — just another word for plants — must be eradicated and lawns regularly mowed and fed. When you think about it, the chores are more exhausting than looking after a house full of demanding children.

Why can we not allow the garden to grow old along with us? Is gentle decrepitude such a bad thing? I am sure the birds and insects that abound in bush gardens would not regard it so. Are we being conned into leaving our much-loved homes, because of the dread words 'the garden is getting too much for you'?

Let us look at alternatives. If in our retirement years (and an enormous number of gardeners are retirees) or earlier, we start to plan a garden that can grow semi-wild, then years of enjoyment can be had without back-breaking toil. Instead of lawns, why not plant trees or shrubs, leaving areas of open space covered in leaf litter, with informal pathways winding through? Shrubs, allowed to grow and spread themselves comfortably, provide shelter for little birds and are a source of visual interest. Perennials give a bounty of flowers each year, but the glory of annuals is a trap for those who are trying to cut down on hard work.

It is difficult to relinquish the idea of an ordered garden, but a garden allowed a natural order can be equally satisfying. Some lovely effects can come about more by chance than good management. Many self-sown plants, particularly reeds and grasses, with their flower plumes and nodding seed heads, bestow a particular charm on an unordered garden.

We need to look for plants that are hardy, well adapted to our climate and soil and long-lived, which will not require endless food, drink and cossetting. Having planted these sturdy friends, we can sit back in our old age and enjoy each other's company.

In whatever region we live, there are National Parks to give us inspiration. In the Mallee country of south-eastern Australia there is an explosion of colourful flowers in the spring. Two-

Bush garden view.

Child at the pond.

thirds of the Mallee country has been cleared for agriculture and two hundred of the original one thousand plant species have been lost or are endangered, which is a compelling reason for trying to save remnants of existing flora on the road verges. National Parks do much to conserve tracts of precious land, but much can be done by individuals to revegetate the degraded areas with indigenous species.

There are large numbers of flowers that thrive in near desert conditions and this should encourage those of us who would like to cut down on watering to try growing them. Water is a precious resource which we use with profligate abandon.

Bush gardens of the desert, the rainforest, the mountains and the coastal regions, all have an individual appeal, and the planting of indigenous species in your garden helps to recreate a vanishing environment. Not only will you grow to love your garden and find it a source of daily refreshment, but it will be appreciated by the birds, butterflies, insects and reptiles, a mini Garden of Eden, without the attendant restraints!

'Come forth into the light of things,
Let Nature be your teacher.'

said the poet Wordsworth and surely this is wise advice for us all to follow.

Epilogue

Silver gulls in flight.

W HEN PETER, MY LIFELONG LOVE AND FRIEND DIED, I felt a crushing sense of desolation and loss and the garden, which is often regarded as a source of solace at such a time, gave me no comfort. In a strange sort of way it seemed heartless in its heedless beauty and unmoved by my loneliness.

Resisting the suggestions of caring friends to move, I stayed on in my home, feeling that to leave would be a betrayal both of all the lovely ploys we had undertaken together and the memories that the garden held for me.

Now, some years later, I am glad that I didn't leave. The garden is a source of joy, the birds are my daily companions and the seasons in their infinite variety continue to unfold their magic.

Appendix:

A list of birds seen in or over the garden

Australian magpie
Australian magpie lark
Australian raven

blackbird
boobook owl
brown thornbill
brush bronze-wing

common bronze-wing
crimson rosella

eastern rosella
eastern shrike tit
eastern spinebill
eastern yellow robin

fairy martin
fantail cuckoo

gang-gang
golden whistler
goshawk
grey butcherbird
grey fantail
grey shrike thrush

kookaburra

little thornbill
little wattlebird

mistletoe bird

New Holland honeyeater

pallid cuckoo

rainbow lorikeet
red-browed finch
red wattlebird
restless flycatcher
rufous fantail
rufous whistler

silvereye
silver gull
spoonbill
spotted pardalote
spotted turtledove
starling
striated pardalote
striated thornbill
sulphur-crested cockatoo
superb blue wren

tawny frogmouth

wedge-tailed eagle
weebill
white-browed scrub wren
white-eared honeyeater
white-faced heron
white ibis
white-naped honeyeater
white-plumed honeyeater
white-throated tree creeper
willie wagtail

yellow-faced honeyeater

Index to Plant Common Names

Index

Sundew.

THE HYLAND HOUSE GARDENING LIBRARY

Quality Books on the Australian Garden
from Australia's Top Garden Writers

GWEN ELLIOT

The New Australian Plants for Small Gardens & Containers
Her complete guide to the use of Australian native plants for gardeners with a
limited amount of space. Fully illustrated hardback with colour plates.
ISBN 0 947062 25 4, $29.95.

Australian Plants for Art & Craft: A Gardener's Handbook
The useful and idea-packed guide to the myriad uses of our native flora—for
decoration, dyes, baskets, fragrant oils and much, much more . . . Fully
illustrated paperback with colour plates. ISBN 0 947062 94 7, $24.95.

SANDRA CLAYTON

The Reverse Garbage Garden
Her highly readable, no-nonsense guide to 'use-everything' gardening. Growing
a garden full of organic vegetables has never been so easy. Fully illustrated
paperback with colour plates. ISBN 1 875657 12 6, $19.95.

The Reverse Garbage Mulch Book
Perhaps the most comprehensive guide to mulching ever compiled, showing
dozens of different mulch materials and mulching methods. Fully illustrated
paperback with colour plates. ISBN 1 875657 40 1, $16.95.

JENNY SMITH

In the Garden with Jenny Smith
A month by month guide to home gardening from one of Australia's most
popular garden writers and broadcasters. Fully illustrated paperback with
colour plates. ISBN 1 875657 15 0, $24.95.

SARAH GUEST

Flowers for the Australian Cottage Garden Border
'A handsome book, with plenty of very practical information including some
good plant lists, full of beautiful illustrations and photographs' Shirley
Stackhouse, *Sydney Morning Herald*. Fully illustrated hardback with colour
plates. ISBN 0 947062 47 5, $35.00.

Flowers from Old Adam's Garden
'Solid information, odd tips, humour and gardening folklore combine . . . to
prove that worthwhile gardening books don't necessarily need glorious colour
photography or boring how-to-do-it instructions.' Anne Latreille, *The Age*.
Fully illustrated hardback. ISBN 0 947062 83 1, $29.95.

ROSEMARY DAVIES

The Creative Gardener's Companion for Australian & New Zealand Gardens
'For the novice who is attempting to make a new garden or renovate an old
one I would, quite unhesitatingly, say that this is the best book they could buy'
Tim North, *Australian Garden Journal*. Fully illustrated hardback with colour
plates. ISBN 0 947062 12 2, $39.95.

Your Garden Questions Answered
All the answers to the most commonly asked garden queries from the popular
ABC garden panellist. Paperback with colour plates.
ISBN 0 947062 81 5, $19.95.